The Government Manager's Guide to Strategic Planning

The Government Manager's Essential Library

The Government Manager's Essential Library is a series of easy-to-use, subject-specific guides on issues every government manager faces:

1. *The Government Manager's Guide to Appropriations Law*, William G. Arnold, CDFM-A

2. *The Government Manager's Guide to Source Selection*, Charles D. Solloway, Jr., CPCM

3. *The Government Manager's Guide to Contract Negotiation*, LeGette McIntyre

4. *The Government Manager's Guide to Plain Language*, Judith Gillespie Myers, Ph.D.

5. *The Government Manager's Guide to the Work Breakdown Structure*, Gregory T. Haugan, Ph.D., PMP

6. **The Government Manager's Guide to Strategic Planning, Kathleen E. Monahan**

7. *The Government Manager's Guide to Project Management*, Jonathan Weinstein, PMP, and Timothy Jaques, PMP

8. *The Government Manager's Guide to Leading Teams*, Lisa DiTullio

9. *The Government Manager's Guide to Earned Value Management*, Charles I. Budd, PMP, and Charlene S. Budd, Ph.D., CPA, CMA, CFM, PMP

10. *The Government Manager's Guide to the Statement of Work*, Michael G. Martin, PMP

11. *The Government Manager's Guide to Contract Law*, Terrence O'Connor

The Government Manager's Guide to Strategic Planning

KATHLEEN E. MONAHAN

MANAGEMENTCONCEPTS PRESS

𝖋𝖋𝖋
MANAGEMENTCONCEPTS PRESS

8230 Leesburg Pike, Suite 800
Tysons Corner, VA 22182
(703) 790-9595
Fax: (703) 790-1371
www.managementconcepts.com

Printed in the United States of America

Library of Congress Control Number: 2013943377

ISBN 978-1-56726-413-5

Portions of this book have been adapted with permission from *Balanced Measures for Strategic Planning: A Public Sector Handbook* by Kathleen E. Monahan, © 2001 by Management Concepts, Inc. All rights reserved.

ABOUT THE AUTHOR

Kathleen E. Monahan, M.A., served with the federal government for 32 years, retiring from the Department of Homeland Security in 2007. During her service, she worked for the Office of the Chief Financial Officer (Department of Housing and Urban Development) and the Immigration and Naturalization Service (Department of Justice) and was one of the first employees of the Department of Homeland Security, serving within the Directorate of Border and Transportation Security. She was also project director for the report *Balancing Measures: Best Practices in Performance Management* for the National Partnership for Reinventing Government, which led to her previous book, *Balanced Measures for Strategic Planning*.

CONTENTS

PREFACE

If you ask people in leadership positions whether they do strategic planning, they will answer that of course they do. Ask them whether they practice performance management, and the answer will usually be yes. However, if you ask those same individuals to describe *how* they do strategic planning or performance management, the answers will be as varied as the people themselves. Strategic planning deals with long-term goals and objectives; performance management—focusing on the performance of an organization, department, employee, or process—is what makes strategic planning work. Neither can be done without the other, but both must be adapted to the organization.

For purposes of this book, performance management deals with organizational performance management, rather than management of individuals or processes. For clarification, individual performance management relates to such things as developing, monitoring, rating, and rewarding employees. Organizational performance management is concerned with performance-based or performance-oriented approaches to managing, measuring, and accounting for an organization's program performance. While individual and organizational concepts should be integrated, they are distinct in some respects, particularly with regard to establishing individual accountability.

Traditionally, most public-sector organizations have measured their organizational performance by focusing on internal or process performance, looking at factors such as the number of positions allotted, the number of programs controlled, or the size of the budget for the fiscal year. By contrast, private-sector businesses have focused on the financial measures of their bottom line: return on investment, market share, and earnings per share.

Alone, neither of these approaches provides the full perspective on an organization's performance that a manager needs to manage effectively. But by balancing internal and process measures with results and financial measures, managers find they have a more complete picture and know where to make improvements.

Robert S. Kaplan and David P. Norton introduced the Balanced Scorecard (BSC) in the early 1990s. Measures established using this concept give managers a comprehensive view of their organization's performance and include both process and results measures. Kaplan and Norton compare the BSC to the dials and indicators in an airplane cockpit. For the complex task of flying an airplane, pilots need detailed information about fuel, air speed, altitude, bearing, and other indicators that summarize the current and predicted environment. Reliance on one instrument can be fatal. By the same token, the variety of problems that arise in the management of an organization requires managers to be able to view performance in several areas at the same time. A BSC or a balanced set of measures provides that valuable information.

The balanced approach gives management a framework that turns business strategy into action by communicating strategic intent to the entire organization and motivating employees through measurement of key performance indicators. Thus, with a "scorecard" on the desktop, a manager can monitor business performance against established targets on all levels of the organization.

The philosophy behind a balanced approach is simple: Set targets and measure the performance related to strategic and operational objectives. In developing these objectives and measures, work with those affected by the activities of your organization to determine what means the most to them. Involve employees. Talk to stakeholders and customers. As an employee of a public-sector organization, the manager should keep in mind that there is a public governance responsibility to the taxpayer as well.

To do all of this correctly, the organization must develop a balanced picture of the organization, focusing on financial as well as nonfinancial, internal as well as external, and performance as well as outcome measures. To implement a balanced approach successfully, the manager must

- Obtain a commitment from organizational leadership and be sure that leadership cascades throughout the organization. If leadership commitment focuses solely on the administration of a public-sector organization, it will shift with elections and have no sustainability. Careerists, as well as political appointees, have to be committed to the process.

- Allow the organization to define strategic objectives and key performance indicators. Work with the employees. Public-sector employees are dedicated individuals who know what they need to do their jobs correctly.

- Involve stakeholders, customers, and employees. Consultation—extensive and ongoing—is a must.

- Develop a communication plan. Communication is key to the process. Without it, the efforts of a public-sector organization become isolated from those who are affected by its activities.

- Use technology to collect, analyze, and use performance information. Don't be afraid to spend the time and money to do it right; it will be worth it.

This book does not purport to be a textbook on the subject of strategic planning, but rather a reference book of ideas for those involved in the day-to-day struggle with performance management and measurement. Remember to adapt, don't adopt—nothing is an exact fit, because all organizations are different. Use what works for you, and leave the rest behind.

My hope is that this book will provide managers with best practices and new ideas to try as we all find our way toward improved performance and accountability for the public sector.

—*Kathleen Monahan*

ACKNOWLEDGMENTS

Special thanks to Myra Strauss, for her unending patience and, with much love, to my husband for his patience while I put this together; to my parents, who inspired me to achieve; and to my "children" (whether you call me Mom or Mama Murph), but most especially to my daughter, Elizabeth, and her daughter—my granddaughter, Lillian.

Chapter 1

AN INTRODUCTION TO STRATEGIC PLANNING

Planning is planning, right? Not really. In fact, there are all kinds of plans and all kinds of planning and planning approaches. All of these approaches and types may be in play at any one time within an organization. Any organization will have plans at different levels, from the five-year (or more) plan to the weekly plan for a project or program.

While working for the Department of Homeland Security, I once sent out a memorandum to department components requesting copies of their "plans." I received a call back from one component informing me that if I wanted all their "plans," I would need an extra building for storage. They had their five-year strategic plan, their annual plans (strategic and budget), operational plans, and tactical plans for specific long-term goals, with interim goals.

This handbook provides guidance for strategic planning in the public sector and advocates an approach that balances performance and financial measures. That doesn't mean that some of the practices discussed can't be adapted to other types of planning. They can be. As I advise later in this book, *adapt, don't adopt*. No concept or practice fits every organization perfectly, so always think about how to adapt a practice to your organization's specific culture and structure or to your specific planning needs.

WHAT IS STRATEGIC PLANNING?

Strategic planning is a process that defines an organization's long-term direction. The process includes a *vision statement* describing where and what the organization wants to be. The *mission statement* defines what the organization is mandated to do. The plan that results from this process and that moves the organization from where it is to where its vision statement wants it to be is a *strategic plan*. It can be broken down into shorter-term, more specific goals, usually with a one-year time frame. The strategic plan is revisited and re-evaluated on a rotational basis, annually or every few years, depending on the organization. Most strategic plans cover the next three to five years.

The strategic plan states where an organization is going, how it's going to get there, and how it will know if it got there. The way a strategic plan is developed depends on the nature of the leadership, the culture of the organization, and the structure and size of the organization. For example, a massive federal department will have multiple planning efforts by smaller organizations within it, resulting in a series of smaller plans that in turn result in a single departmental strategic plan. A smaller organization with a single focus, such as a local fire or police department, will have a less complicated process. (The strategic planning process is discussed in more detail in Chapter 3.)

Manager Alert

The way a strategic plan is developed depends on the nature of the leadership, the culture of the organization, and the structure and size of the organization.

An organization must first answer two questions before any strategic planning process can begin:

1. **What, exactly, do we do—and NOT do?** In the public sector, this can be a very complicated question. Over a period of time, "mission creep" sometimes occurs—when an organization begins to take on responsibilities that are not part of its official mandate.

    In seeking the answer, the planning process should include asking management to write down what they do, then having them define under what mandate (e.g., a law, an executive order, or perhaps a congressional unfunded mandate) they do it. Never, ever settle for the answer "we do it because we always have." This process should result in a mission statement.

2. **Who are our partners, stakeholders, and customers?** Begin by identifying partner, stakeholder, and customer roles, as well as each group's expectations. Roles should be defined as specifically as possible during the planning process. There will always be some crossover among these three groups; it is possible for someone to be both a stakeholder and a customer.

    This question can be answered through consultation efforts (discussed in Chapters 2 and 3). Consultation will also help define outcomes and goals. This consultation activity, and all resulting discussions, are the *consultation phase*.

In addition to answering these fundamental questions, the planning process should include the following activities:

- Defining an end state for the organization—whether five, ten, or more years out—that results in a vision statement
- Establishing long-term and short-term goals
- Allocating resources to achieve both the long-term and the short-term goals
- Understanding the current status
- Communicating goals and plan back to the customer, stakeholder, and partner.

A second consultation phase helps focus the proposed goals. This should be continual throughout the process until the goals and plan are finalized.

Strategic Planning in the Public Sector

The Government Performance and Results Act (GPRA) brought private-sector accounting concepts to government agencies. When it was first implemented in the 1990s, many felt that government management was somehow different—that the same rules that applied to the private sector could not apply to the public sector, or at least not in the same way, and compliance with GPRA was "beneath" them. After all, government agencies don't have a bottom line or profit margin. But history has shown that this assumption is not true. The bottom line for most government organizations is their mission—what they want to achieve.

Manager Alert

The bottom line for most government organizations is their mission—what they want to achieve.

Like the private sector, they cannot achieve this mission by managing in a vacuum. The roles of customer, partner, stakeholder, and employee in an organization's day-to-day operations are vital to its success—and must be incorporated into planning for that success.

The history of strategic planning in the public sector began on separate paths that eventually merged. The private sector experimented for several years with different types of performance management and measurement. These include, among others, Management by Objective, Zero Based Budgeting, and Total Quality Management (TQM). As these various practices began to demonstrate significant improvement for private-sector entities, state and local governments began to experiment with them. Frequently led by elected officials with private-sector experience, these governments soon began to develop better communication and management systems.

Federal-sector organizations also began experimenting, especially with Zero Based Budgeting and Total Quality Management. The United States Coast Guard acknowledges that its experience with TQM paved the way for its highly successful continuous improvement and performance efforts today.

Legislation in the late 1980s and early 1990s began to move the federal sector toward more responsible performance management and measurement. Among the laws and regulations that formed the basis for public-sector strategic planning were the following:

- **Federal Managers Financial Integrity Act of 1982, Public Law 97-255.** Commonly referred to as "FMFIA," the act encompasses accounting and financial management programs and operational and administrative areas and establishes specific requirements for management controls in federal agencies. Agency heads must establish controls that responsibly ensure that (1) obligations and costs comply with applicable law; (2) assets are safeguarded against waste, loss, unauthorized use, or misappropriation; and (3) revenues and expenditures are properly recorded and accounted for in accordance with the law. Additionally, agency heads must annually evaluate and report on the control and financial systems that protect the integrity of federal programs.

- **Chief Financial Officers Act of 1990, Public Law 101-576.** The CFO Act of 1990 was enacted to improve the financial management practices of the federal government and to ensure the production of reliable and timely financial information for use in managing and evaluating federal programs.

- **Government Management Reform Act of 1994, Public Law 103-356.** GMRA furthered the objectives of the CFO Act by requiring all federal agencies to prepare and publish annual financial reports, beginning with fiscal year 1996 activities. At the same time, GMRA authorized the Office of Management and Budget to implement a pilot program to streamline and consolidate certain statutory financial management and performance reports into a single, annual accountability report.

- **Government Performance and Results Act of 1993, Public Law 103-62.** GPRA is the primary legislative framework through which agencies are required to set strategic goals, measure performance, and report on the degree to which goals were met. It requires each federal agency to develop strategic plans and a subsequent annual performance plan to provide the direct link between the strategic goals outlined in the agency's strategic plan and the day-to-day operations of managers and employees. GPRA requires that each agency submit an annual report on program performance for the previous fiscal year, reviewing and discussing its performance compared with the performance goals it established in its annual performance plan. The report also evaluates the agency's performance plan for the fiscal year in which the performance report was submitted to show how an agency's actual performance is influencing its plans.

- **Executive Order 12862: Setting Customer Service Standards, September 11, 1993.** This executive order puts "people first . . . ensuring that the Federal Government provides the highest quality service possible to the American people." It requires continual reform of the executive branch's management practices and operations to provide service to the public that matches or exceeds the best service available in the private sector. All executive departments and agencies are required to "establish and implement customer service standards to guide the operations" of each agency and to "provide significant services directly to the public . . . in a manner that seeks to meet the customer service standard established herein." They are also required to report on Customer Service Surveys and Customer Service Plans.

- **Presidential Memorandum for Heads of Executive Departments and Agencies: Improving Customer Service, March 23, 1995.** With "Setting Customer Service Standards" as the first phase, this presidential memorandum directs that, to continue customer service reform, agencies shall treat the requirements of the earlier executive order as continuing requirements. The purpose is to establish and implement customer service standards that will guide the operations of the executive branch. "Services" include those provided directly to the public, delivered in partnership with state and local governments by small agencies, regulatory agencies, and enforcement agencies. Results achieved are measured against the customer service standards and reported annually. Customer views determine whether standards have been met on what matters most to the customer, and replacement standards will be published, if needed, to reflect these views. Development and tracking are to be integrated with other performance initiatives. Customer service standards should relate to legislative activities, including GPRA, the CFO Act, and GMRA. Employees are to be surveyed on ideas to improve customer service and will be recognized for meeting or exceeding customer service standards. An important observation is made within this memorandum: "Without satisfied employees, we cannot have satisfied customers." It is also recommended that agencies initiate and support actions that cross agency lines to serve shared customer groups and take steps to develop cross-agency, one-stop service to customer groups.

- **Information Technology Management Reform Act of 1996 (also known as the Clinger-Cohen Act or the CIO Act), Public Law 104-106.** This act repeals Section 111 of the Federal Property and Administrative Services Act of 1949 (40 U.S.C. 759), often referred to as the Brooks Act, and gives the General Services Administration exclusive authority to acquire computer resources for all of the federal government. It assigns overall responsibility for the acquisition and management of information technology (IT) in the federal government to the Director of the Office of Management and Budget (OMB). It also gives the authority to acquire IT resources to the heads of each executive agency and makes them responsible for effectively managing their IT investments. The primary purposes of the bill are to streamline IT acquisitions and emphasize life cycle management of IT as a capital investment. The key IT management actions are to require agency heads to design and implement an IT management process, integrate it with the other organizational processes, establish goals for improving the efficiency and effectiveness of agency operations, deliver services to the public through the effective use of IT, prepare an annual report on the progress in achieving the goals, appoint a Chief Information Officer, and inventory all computer equipment and identify any excess equipment.

- **Government Performance and Results Modernization Act of 2010, Public Law 111–352**

  GPRA 2010 created a more clearly defined performance framework through an improved governance structure and by connecting plans, programs, and performance information. It requires a quarterly (rather than annual) reporting and review process. This report/review cycle was designed to increase the use of performance information in program decision-making.

  There are three key revisions to requirements in the legislation:

  1. Timing of agency strategic planning was changed to align with presidential terms of office. Cross-agency alignment of goals and programs was added as a requirement, and *congressional consultation* was more clearly defined.

  2. A mandate requiring a link between the performance goals in the annual plan and the goals in the strategic plans was added. It requires that plans describe strategies and resources to be used and requires plans to cover a two-year period (rather than a one-year period).

  3. Agency performance reporting requirements emphasized more regular reporting. More importantly for federal agencies, it required OMB to take action on agency unmet goals.

In addition to the above, GPRA 2010 validated the existing governance framework that had evolved since the original GPRA was passed. It created chief operating officers, program improvement officers, a governmentwide performance improvement council, and a governmentwide performance website.

New, focused requirements under these various laws and regulations caused managers to rethink how they planned their activities and how they defined success. The one law that made a more powerful impact on this area than any other was GPRA, which set a schedule for the development of a strategic planning process for all segments of the federal government. The need for federal agencies to develop systems for performance management and measurement began a chain reaction, particularly for those agencies whose principal customers or stakeholders are state and local governments.

State and local governments that had already put systems into place were ahead of the game. Those that had not were (or in some cases are now) put into the position of catching up with the others. In a sense, this sequence has given new life to the concept of *best practices*. There has been a significant amount of give and take between the various levels of government. A community of practice that allows leaders at every level of public service to learn from the experience of others has evolved.

HISTORY OF THE BALANCED APPROACH

In the early 1990s, Robert S. Kaplan and David P. Norton introduced the concept of the Balanced Scorecard (BSC) to the private sector. (For further information on the work of Kaplan and Norton, please refer to their website, www.bcol.com.) Their groundbreaking *Harvard Business Review* article (January 1992) and subsequent works discuss private-sector efforts to align corporate initiatives with the need to meet customer and shareholder expectations.

A BSC is an organizational tool that translates an organization's mission strategy into objectives and measures organized into four different perspectives: financial, customer, internal business process, and learning and growth (Figure 1-1). It provides all employees with information they can use to achieve the organization's goals.

At about the same time, Karl Sveiby was introducing the concept of the Intangible Assets Monitor (IAM) to the private sector in countries outside the United States. Both concepts create indicators that measure aspects of business and assume that the performance of an organization should be measured by more than merely the "bottom line." Although they appear similar, the two concepts were developed independently, and the theories behind them differ.

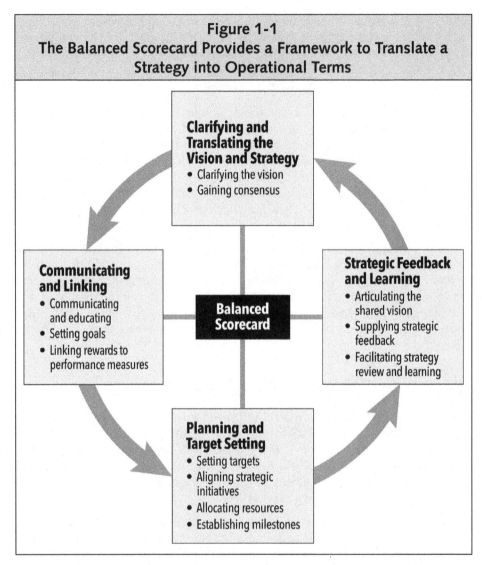

Figure 1-1
The Balanced Scorecard Provides a Framework to Translate a Strategy into Operational Terms

Source: Robert S. Kaplan and David P. Norton, "Using the Balanced Scorecard as a Strategic Management System," *Harvard Business Review* (January-February 1996): 76. Reprinted with permission.

The IAM sets forth the idea that human knowledge has very little to do with money, since very few people in an organization handle money. If the source of revenue is an organization's employees, a planner must come closer to "the source" of their knowledge to measure it more accurately. By measuring closer to the source, it becomes possible to create an early warning system for failure to achieve goals more oriented to the future than one that relies on the financial accounting system. For this reason, the IAM argues that nonfinancial indicators are probably superior to financial ones. It focuses primarily on three intangible assets (external structure, internal structure, and individual competence) and acknowledges that financial indicators already exist within the strategy of the organization.

The BSC, on the other hand, sets forth the idea that to develop a long-term plan, organizational leaders must strive to balance four separate but intertwined aspects of the organization's environment. Doing otherwise could produce success in the short term but would ultimately result in long-term failure. Unlike traditional measurement systems, based solely on financial information, the BSC sets objectives and measures performance from four distinct perspectives that are equally important: customer satisfaction, internal business, learning and growth, and the financial perspective. Together, these perspectives provide a balanced view of the present and future performance of the business.

BSC users are likely to develop nonfinancial indicators that are different from those used with the IAM and that also will be interpreted differently. The IAM assumes that some of the organization's assets are intangible, and its purpose is to guide managers in how to utilize those assets while increasing, renewing, and guarding them against the risk of loss. The IAM is thus more similar to traditional accounting theory, with its balance sheet and income statements, than the BSC. The BSC begins from the base of a traditional management information system and adds three nonfinancial perspectives to that system.

While the IAM is based on the "knowledge perspective" of a firm, the BSC regards the perspective of the firm as a given, urging managers to take a more balanced view. In their 1996 book, Kaplan and Norton state: "The Balanced Scorecard complements financial measures of past performance with measures of the drivers of future performance. The objectives and measures of the scorecard are derived from an organization's vision and strategy."[1] That strategy is then translated into action through the planning documents.

APPLICATION OF A BALANCED APPROACH TO THE PUBLIC SECTOR

As a result of these two concepts, a need evolved to study in-depth how all these efforts related to the public sector and if they could be replicated there. Could federal, state, and local government entities improve their strategic planning efforts by including customers, stakeholders, and employees in their processes? What would it take to reach some balance between the needs and opinions of these groups and the achievement of the organization's stated mission?

A balanced approach in the public sector must look at four areas of responsibility, some of which correspond to the original concepts of the BSC: public governance, operational, supporting, and client responsibilities.[2]

Public Governance Responsibilities

Public governance responsibilities address how we should appear to our customers and stakeholders as policy and resource stewards. The mission of the organization must align itself with its legislative mandates, which will provide the basic information. For the federal sector, congressional consultation is especially vital. Consultation with stakeholders is critical to this process and will identify their key needs and requirements, which can then be integrated into the overall planning process. Duplicate or multiple programs can sometimes be integrated through this process as well. Closely analyzing exactly what the organization must achieve and focusing on the mission can clarify expectations for everyone—stakeholder, customer, employee, and the organization as a whole.

As you, the government manager, look for the best policy results and achievement of mission, keep in mind that you are enacting legislative language. Are the mandated policies effectively translated into goals for implementation? Are you also addressing the fiduciary responsibilities of the organization? In a time of severe budget restraints, it is important to communicate the financial and performance restraints clearly (e.g., an agency is trying to downsize, and there will be fewer individuals to achieve a mission). Figure 1-2 maps out the three phases of strategic planning: (1) defining the mission of the organization; (2) developing the goals, objectives, and indicators; and (3) using performance information for a continuous improvement process. In day-to-day operations, continuous improvement allows combining decision-making with accountability, creating incentives, and building expertise. The four areas of responsibility for a public-sector organization provide the guidelines for your decisions in this process.

Manager Alert

As you look for the best policy results and achievement of mission, keep in mind that you are enacting legislative language.

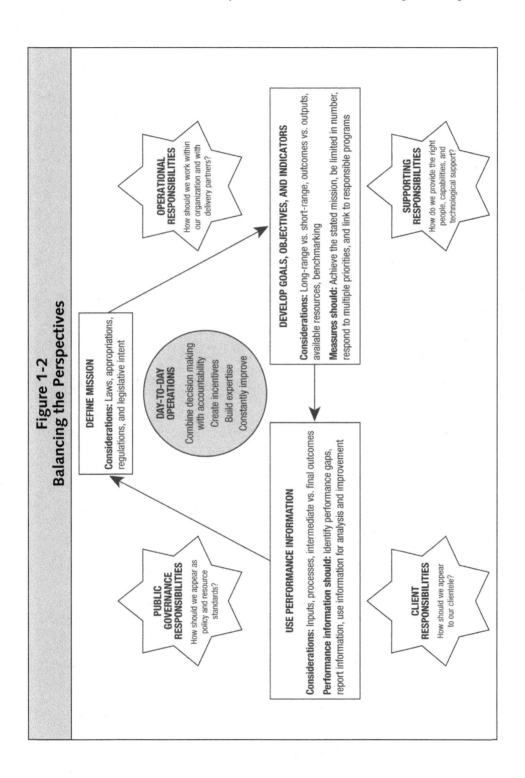

Figure 1-2
Balancing the Perspectives

Operational Responsibilities

Operational responsibilities are how we work within our organizations as well as with delivery partners, such as state and local governments, to achieve our stated mission. To be successful in this area, we must understand and measure (e.g., for time, cost, quality, and quantity) the core processes and their value chains. A value chain in the private sector defines all of the activities and processes an organization performs while producing a product. In the public sector, a value chain analysis helps an agency provide a service that is of value to the citizens it serves. Value chain analysis defines each particular activity in terms of the value added to the organization's products or services. The overall concept is that an organization is more than a random set of things. Rather, for the organization to be efficient and effective, the individual items must be arranged into systems and processes. For more on value chains, see Chapter 2.

This is an area where "stovepiping" does the most harm. *Stovepiping* refers to limited or nonexistent communication among individual areas within an organization. Programs are managed solely in terms of their impact on the program—that is, within their own cylinder or stove pipe—rather than in terms of impact on the organization as a whole. (In Brazilian culture, management planners refer to a program having "its own church.")

As the BSC takes hold, particularly in the federal sector, we frequently hear about "one" organization, e.g. "One HUD" or "One DHS." This concept of one organization reflects an emphasis on establishment of cross-program and even cross-bureau goals and objectives, rather than multiple individual goals. In some areas where this has been successful, the emphasis is now shifting to interagency outcomes for future planning cycles.

The emphasis should be on comprehensive processes and interrelationships. Process mapping can be a great help here. Process owners must be identified and held accountable for the results. Does an organization have delivery partners? Where do they fit into the achievement of its mission? Does the service or benefit go directly to the citizen, or does the funding go through an intermediary source? When you map the processes, you must include delivery partners and supplier roles.

Customer consultation played an important role in the development of customer-related indicators for the St. Lawrence Seaway Management Corporation (SLSMC). By agreement with users, certain types of delays (e.g., fog) are not included to calculate transit time achievement. In establishing goals, a "norm" transit time was established, i.e., within normal conditions, as the optimum time to go from Point A to Point B. Transit time targets of 90% transit within norm + 2 hours and 95% transit within norm + 4 hours were then agreed on. SLSMC and its customers review the results and targets yearly and adjust them if necessary.

Supporting Responsibilities

Supporting responsibilities are the responsibilities we have to our employees. Do we have the right people? How do we, as an organization, provide them with the training, capabilities, and technological support they must have to do the job correctly and deliver high-quality service to the customer?

Client Responsibilities

Client responsibilities address how we want to (or should) appear to those outside the organization. The term as used here encompasses not only customers in the traditional sense but also indirect recipients of services or benefits and the ultimate customer: the taxpayer. In meeting these client responsibilities, balancing can become more like juggling—there may never be a time when everyone affected by a particular program will be in total agreement. A *client* is not always a *customer*, because some organizations regulate as well as provide a benefit or service. The client, too, has some level of responsibility in the achievement of successful results.

Communication among the groups can help define the limitations of the public-sector organization, especially for the recipient of the service. The expectations of an individual receiving a benefit or service may be beyond the capabilities of the organization. There must be balance between what the recipient, as a customer, wants and what the organization can provide while maintaining its responsibilities to the taxpayer. Communication can become critical—honesty regarding limitations vs. expectations allows "opposing" sides to understand the strategic planning issues with which the organization is struggling. The client groups, clearly defined, need to be involved in defining goals, targets, and strategies.

Manager Alert

Although a communications campaign can be waged on an *ad hoc* basis, an organization will get a better return on its investment if the activities are undertaken within a strategic framework.

Where does financial measurement fit into this scenario? Although public-sector organizations do not exist to make a profit, they do have a fiduciary responsibility to achieve their mission in a cost-efficient manner. In today's world of tighter budget restraints, this has gained additional importance. Measurement of these responsibilities is most clearly defined in such legislation as the Chief Financial Officers Act, the Government Management Reform Act, and the Clinger-Cohen Act. GPRA, too, requires linking budgetary resources with strategic planning efforts. However, financial performance is not the only area that crosses from private sector to public sector.

Customer satisfaction is particularly important to public-sector organizations, since one of the customers—the taxpayer—is also the source of funding. While in the private sector, internal efficiency would not generally be of concern to the customer, efficiency and productivity are of great concern to government customers, as they are paying for the service. For this reason, internal efficiency, also referred to as cost-effectiveness, should be a key element in strategic planning in the public sector.

Successful organizations believe that, while there is no perfect fit within the public sector for either the BSC as envisioned by Kaplan and Norton or the IAM, the overall concept can nevertheless be useful in government planning—particularly with some tinkering and tailoring. For example, public-sector organizations with the most mature strategic planning processes—notably, city and state governments—feel that the area of employee satisfaction translates better to the public sector when viewed as employee empowerment or involvement.

Some important lessons to remember about balancing performance measurement include

- **Adapt, don't adopt.** Make a best practice work for you. Each organization, whether public or private, has its own unique culture. Take the best practices and adapt them to your specific organizational culture—don't try to force what worked in another place onto your organization without taking that uniqueness into account.

- **We aren't so different after all.** Whether public or private, federal, state, or local, there are common problems and common answers. Defining who the customer is may be less of a challenge for the private sector; otherwise, the issues are markedly similar: opening and maintaining solid lines of communication with your customers, stakeholders, and employees; achieving organizational goals in a cost-effective and efficient manner; and making sure your product, service, or benefit is the best possible.

- **Leadership doesn't stop at the top.** It should cascade through an organization, creating champions and a team approach to achievement of the mission. In a public-sector organization, the political leadership will shift with elections. If the head of a department really wants to make a lasting difference, the overall process needs to become an integral part of the organization, not just a product produced by the head office or contractor. If the process is part of the entire organization, it will attain an enduring sustainability.

- **Listen to your customers, your stakeholders, your employees, and unions.** This doesn't mean send out surveys, collect the paperwork, and put it in some fancy notebook on a shelf in the office. It means communicate with them. Be prepared to listen to what they have to say and to act on it.

- **Partnership means success.** Don't tell customers, stakeholders, and employees what they need. *Ask* them—it works much better.

Manager Alert
Listen to your customers, your stakeholders, your employees, and unions.

WHY A BALANCED APPROACH WORKS

Why should you, a government leader, try to achieve a balanced set of performance measures, or what's often referred to as a *family* of measures? Because your job is to meet your customer's expectations and fulfill your organization's mission. In other words . . .

You need to know your customer's expectations and your employee's needs

Define what service or benefit the customer wants and what the employee needs to deliver that service or benefit. No organization can achieve a mission without the tools to accomplish its daily responsibilities, so human resource systems should use employee surveys. Necessary skills and competencies must be determined through analysis. Once those have been determined, then a curriculum of training can be developed. Management tools, such as appraisals, should align stated goals with actual performance. Workforce size and productivity issues, as well as access to information and technology, are also factors to consider. The resulting organizational culture should support the entire workforce in achievement of its mission.

You must plan for those expectations and needs to achieve your stated objectives

The success of the organization is determined in large part by the involvement of individual employees in the overall process, their awareness of their roles in the achievement of the mission, and their belief in the vision of the organization. Once the customer and the expectations of service or benefit are defined, there is a basis for discussion with employees. Involving employees is critical because they are your front line with the customer. (For a more thorough discussion of involving the employee, see Chapter 4.)

A balanced approach to performance management *works*

The BSC helps an organization become aligned on one strategy, eliminating the strategy disconnect between leadership and line workers by helping employees understand how they personally can make an impact on the performance of the business. It also allows customers to understand the limitations of an organization and adjust their expectations accordingly. When involved in these discussions, the stakeholder is provided with the full scope of the issues and can work better with the organization toward successful achievement of the mission.

When there is an open line of communication among the organizational leadership, the employee, the customer, and the stakeholder, the entire culture of the organization can change, focusing on achievement of the mission.

With the BSC, a public organization has the necessary tools to decide which projects are most important to the achievement of its goals while becoming more efficient and improving the level of service or benefit it is offering to the customer. Most important, the BSC provides a means of communication for successful implementation of strategic plans and a budget that is performance based.

> If you don't know where you are going, you'll end up someplace else.
>
> — Yogi Berra

NOTES

1. Robert S. Kaplan and David P. Norton, *The Balanced Scorecard: Translating Strategy into Action* (Boston: Harvard Business School Press, 1996), 8.
2. Special thanks to Sharon Caudle, Ph.D., of the GAO for her assistance with this section.

Chapter 2

DETERMINING PUBLIC VALUE: MEETING PUBLIC GOVERNANCE AND CLIENT RESPONSIBILITIES THROUGH CONSULTATION

A s discussed in Chapter 1, the responsibilities of the public-sector organization include public governance and client responsibilities. Every organization has a value that reflects its role in society. In the public sector, that value is defined by the organization's mandate and the perceptions of the customer and stakeholder. Public value is created by the satisfaction of stakeholders (such as Congress and the administration) with the achieved outcome as well as the satisfaction of customers in receiving the desired product, services, or authorization.

For those serving in the federal sector, there is added incentive from the Government Performance and Results Act (GPRA), which requires an assessment of public value. The strategic planning process should be designed to heighten that public value. To assess the value of your public product or service, create and maintain a dialogue—known as *stakeholder consultation*—with all those who have an impact on or are involved in any way with the achievement of your mission, including the customer, stakeholder, and employee (see Figure 2-1).

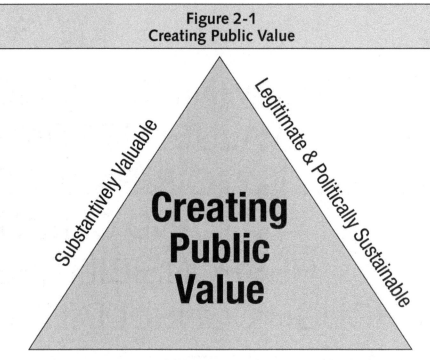

Figure 2-1
Creating Public Value

Substantively Valuable

Legitimate & Politically Sustainable

Creating Public Value

Operationally & Administratively Feasible

Substantively Valuable—Produce things of value to overseers, clients, and beneficiaries at low cost in terms of money and authority

Legitimate & Politically Sustainable—Ability to attract both authority and money from politically authorizing environment to which it is accountable

Operationally & Administratively Feasible—Authorized and valuable activities can be accomplished by the existing organization or in combination with partners

Although GPRA was passed in August 1993, the first required document, the strategic plan, was due in September 1997. Most agencies did not focus on their responsibilities under GPRA until fiscal year 1996. On the federal level, the concept of stakeholder consultation for most agencies was previously limited to meetings with congressional staff. Only a limited number of agencies conducted consultation with customers, stakeholders, and employees.

Most federal agencies make a sincere effort to work with their customers, stakeholders, and employees. The consultation phase of strategic planning has become far more focused in the federal sector as agencies reevaluate their strategic plans and annual performance plans. Legislative support can be a byproduct of a successful consultation process—if the legislature is a partner in that process:

- The states of Texas and Iowa consult extensively with their legislative bodies when developing their priorities.
- GPRA 2010 delineated the importance of consultation with Congress.
- Natural Resources of Canada credits its success in performance measurement to three factors: top management support, intradepartmental collaboration, and consultation with top stakeholders, including the Canadian Parliament.

Public support, created because the client has input into the process, can be highly beneficial when defending budget requests before a legislative body—yet another good reason to communicate openly with the public.

State and local governments, while not subject to GPRA, started before the federal government did and had more time to establish measures; consult with stakeholders, partners, and customers; and then redefine their families of measures as necessary. For example, the city of Austin, Texas, developed a community scorecard that includes measures for public safety, crime control, and neighborhood vitality; support of families; and protection of the environment. It also includes shorter-term measures drawn from customer surveys on topics that were of immediate concern to citizens. This community scorecard is widely available through the local media and the Internet, and the city's current activities may be found at www.austintexas.gov/budget/eperf/index.cfm.

Another local government, the city of Coral Springs, Florida, has developed performance measures that indicate the city's "stock price." The index includes 10 performance measures most critical to the city's customers (as determined by survey), including residential property values, school overcrowding, and crime rate, and an overall customer satisfaction rating. The city reviews its strategic priorities every two years in formal strategic planning workshops. Management as well as frontline employees and volunteers on advisory boards and commissions have input to the process, which includes financial and demographic data and projections, customer surveys on desires and perceptions, customer input as obtained from neighborhood town hall meetings, and—of course—performance results. Additionally, each employee of Coral Springs develops personal objectives that tie back to the city's key intended outcomes, thus connecting them to strategic priorities and ensuring that employees actually understand them. All these interconnected processes create a city with a reputation for being an open and caring community in which to live and work.

THE DIFFERENCE BETWEEN A CUSTOMER AND A STAKEHOLDER

In the public sector, how is the difference between a customer and a stakeholder defined? It is not a simple delineation; the boundaries are not clear, bright lines. The dictionary defines a customer as someone who "purchases goods or services from another." A stakeholder is "a person or group that has an investment, share, or interest in something." Which category should the public be placed in?

Consultation through the use of representative focus groups (see Chapter 3) has met with success in achieving goals that resonate with an organization's customers, stakeholders and partners. These three groups are defined as follows:

- The customer is the direct recipient of an organization's services.
- Stakeholders are usually defined as those people or organizations that have an interest in an organization's products or services and supply resources (such as the Office of Management and Budget and Congress). They have an interest in how the products or services are produced or in the unintended results of delivering them. Stakeholders are, according to most definitions, not actual recipients of the product or service of the organization. For many organizations, taxpayers are defined as stakeholders, rather than customers.
- Partners are those people or organizations (either internal or external) that help an organization deliver its products or services. These include labor unions, universities, state governments, and private industry.

THE VALUE CHAIN

Figure 2-2 shows the value chain for both a public and private-sector organization. Note that the top section of the chain is the same for both organizations, while the variance occurs on the bottom portion of the chain. The private sector focuses on *shareholder value, profitability,* and *customer loyalty,* whereas a public-sector organization has *public trust* instead of customer loyalty, *mission achievement* instead of profitability, and *public value* instead of shareholder value.

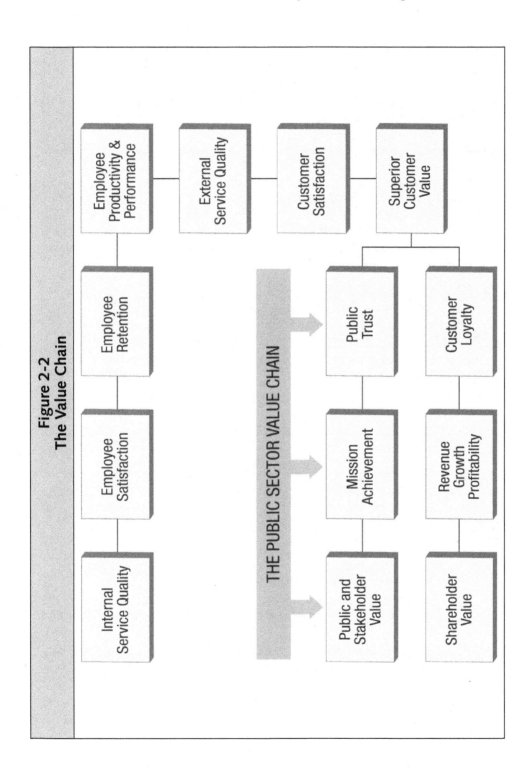

Figure 2-2
The Value Chain

Manager Alert

The private sector focuses on *shareholder value, profitability,* and *customer loyalty,* whereas a public-sector organization has *public trust* instead of customer loyalty, *mission achievement* instead of profitability, and *public value* instead of shareholder value.

The government manager should ask these questions to define the core purpose of an organization (see Table 2-1): Will the successful achievement of your mission create a public value? How do you measure the success of your mission? Do private-sector models for customer value translate to the public sector? What is the fundamental reason for your existence? The answer lies both in your enacting language and in the minds of those you serve.

Table 2-1
Core Purpose = Fundamental Reason for Being

Organization	Purpose
Bureau of Land Management (BLM)	Use and enjoyment of public lands
Forest Service	Care for the land and serve the people
Health and Human Services	To enhance the health and well-being of all Americans
Department of Transportation	Ensure a transportation system that enhances quality of life

In the private sector, major corporations list their core purpose in all their planning documents. Disney will tell you: Our core purpose is to make people happy. For Cargill, it is to improve the standard of living around the world. Hewlett-Packard gives its purpose as "to make technical contributions for the advancement and welfare of humanity." Note the similarities with core purposes in the public sector.

The product or service your organization produces must be

- **Substantively valuable.** It must produce something of value to the beneficiary at a low cost to the government in terms of money and authority.

- **Legitimate and politically sustainable.** It must attract both authority and money from a politically authorizing environment to which is it accountable.

- **Operationally and administratively feasible.** The authorized and valuable activity can be accomplished by the existing organization or in combination with partners.

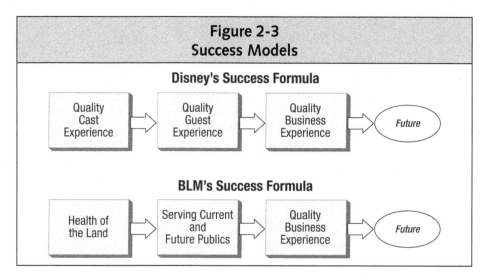

Figure 2-3
Success Models

Disney's Success Formula

Quality Cast Experience → Quality Guest Experience → Quality Business Experience → *Future*

BLM's Success Formula

Health of the Land → Serving Current and Future Publics → Quality Business Experience → *Future*

In seeking future success, seek out those organizations that have already achieved success and determine what they did right. Success models for BLM and Disney (see Figure 2-3) start with priorities specific to each organization, but neither can achieve success without quality business practices. Those quality business practices reflect your public-sector value.

In determining public-sector value, there are three traditional options:

- **Program evaluation**—how well the program achieved its intended purpose)
- **Cost-effectiveness**—how well a particular governmental effort "scored" with respect to a set of purposes and defined effort boundaries
- **Customer satisfaction**—how well the government effort satisfied the needs of the representative citizens and customers.

A well-structured consultation process will use the third option by establishing and maintaining open lines of communication with representative citizens and customers, including employees and stakeholders.

THE CONSULTATION PROCESS

From mission to measures, a critical part of the development of your strategic planning process is to consult with customers to determine what is necessary to satisfy the needs of representative citizens and customers—needs that may be conflicting. These conflicts can be resolved by creating a focus group (see Chapter 3) with representatives from all points of view, including a stakeholder (who knows the mission of the organization) and a facilitator (to keep things focused), and then listening to the exchange of ideas. Such sharing of ideas and opinions, or consultation, can result in fresh new approaches to old problems.

A distinction between citizens who are customers and those who are stakeholders should be made. For our purposes, the customer is the recipient of the benefit or service, and the stakeholder is any individual citizen who is not a direct recipient. To achieve results, do the customer and stakeholder have responsibilities? For example, job training programs are a service provided at many different levels of government. Is it the responsibility of the organization to provide training or to get people jobs? The individual being trained—that is, the customer—has responsibilities as well. A stakeholder, the taxpayer, may wish for the responsibilities of the individual being trained to be clarified.

Stakeholders, such as Congress, may also have expectations based in legislative mandates. Expectations resulting from laws, appropriations, and regulations help define the organization's role in society and the impact of the organization's activities.

Employees know what they need to get the job done. Consulting with them helps define those needs, including alignment of goals and human resource systems, access to information, technology, and training. Employee involvement in the planning process creates an organization based on results, which in turn results in higher levels of employee satisfaction and retention.

Consultation has a significant impact on how the organization's overall performance is managed. If customers, stakeholders, and employees are part of the planning process, they then become part of the achievement as well, building an environment of trust and openness that can make positive changes. The strategic planning process, from establishment to performance reporting, should thus be collaborative and interactive at all levels.

IDENTIFYING YOUR CUSTOMER AND STAKEHOLDER

Defining exactly who the customer is presents a special challenge for government agencies with both an enforcement and service mission, such as the U.S. Coast Guard, because there are essentially two different customer bases. Even regulatory agencies that have a single mission, such as the Environmental Protection Agency, must take into account not only those with whom they deal on a daily basis in their enforcement activities, such as major manufacturers, but also the citizens whom they are protecting with those enforcement activities. And the organization that provides a service or benefit, such as the Social Security Administration, must distinguish between what the customer may want and what U.S. citizens may be willing to spend—that is, to balance their fiscal responsibilities to the taxpayer with their responsibilities to beneficiaries.

Manager Alert

Defining exactly who the customer is presents a special challenge for government agencies with both an enforcement and a service mission.

The first thing you should do is map out the process completely, from when the dollars are authorized by the legislative body until the product or service is delivered to the customer. If you are providing a financial benefit, such as a voucher, does your organization actually produce the voucher, or does the money go from your organization through intermediary organizations to the beneficiary? Each level of intermediary has an interest in your plans for the future, especially how you prioritize your goals and how you plan to measure your achievements. Process mapping serves a number of purposes: (1) clarifying for everyone involved exactly how your program functions; (2) identifying those affected by or involved in your program at every point; and (3) identifying those areas where efficiencies, when combined with any reengineering or reinvention effort, can most easily be implemented.

As a manager, having identified all those involved in the delivery of your service or product, you need to think about how you want to structure your initial consultation sessions. Do you want to have sessions by region, or would you prefer to divide them along issues? Some organizations prefer to organize their larger consultation sessions by an issue, such as welfare-to-work or education. Some federal agencies have held their initial sessions based on a specific strategic goal. Each method has benefits and drawbacks.

If you meet by region, certain areas, such as large cities, may produce such a diverse audience that reaching consensus will be unlikely, if not impossible. In that case, breaking into smaller, more limited groups may be the answer. Avoid holding a session where two large groups with strong opposing views (e.g., a major chemical corporation and an environmental group) are both represented. Putting the two large groups together should be avoided because there is a strong likelihood that the session will be contentious and unproductive. In addition, you want to ensure that the smaller groups and individuals have an opportunity to state their views as well, and not allow the larger group to dominate the session. This is a key role that needs to be clarified with the facilitator.

If you decide in favor of separate sessions with each group, in what order do you want to conduct your meetings? Do you want to talk first with stakeholders, such as OMB, Congress, the state legislature, or local board, and then incorporate their comments and concerns into your proposed plan? Or do you want to meet first with your customers and then take their feedback with you to meet with the stakeholders?

Special interest groups are affected by this decision and may be either stakeholders or customers, depending on how you view their input. Some larger interest groups may be more appropriately considered stakeholders, not only because of the large number of customers they represent, but also because of their ability to affect legislative decisions. For example, if a plan included a goal to reduce gun violence, the National Rifle Association (NRA) would be a stakeholder, as its ability to lobby could make or break your organization's ability to achieve that goal.

Special interest groups represent a type of customer who should be an integral part of the process throughout. A continuing dialogue with them allows the public-sector organization to reach the maximum number of customers in the most efficient manner. They should not, however, become the only contact you have with your customers; rather, you should also allow for individual customer input as well. This is an area where focus groups can come into play.

WHY REGULATORY AND ENFORCEMENT AGENCIES ARE (AND ARE *NOT*) DIFFERENT

Regulatory agencies face a special challenge in establishing and implementing customer measures. In this area more than any other, the concept of customer vs. client (see Chapter 1) comes into play. An individual who is being investigated, regulated, interdicted, inspected, restricted, or audited will hardly be effusive with customer satisfaction. Some regulatory agencies, therefore, are taking a new look at the definition of *customer*, broadening it to include the entire American public. This new focus requires innovative means of assessing satisfaction.

As an example, the U.S. Coast Guard regulates the commercial shipping industry in working toward its strategic goal regarding safety. Shipping companies do not choose to be customers, but because they must comply with Coast Guard regulations and because Coast Guard activities and performance measures are oriented toward safety, they are considered customers.

In a study performed by the National Partnership for Reinventing Government on balanced measures in the public sector, one of the teams within that study (the Regulatory Agencies Team) approached the study with the special orientation such agencies have—a recognition of the challenges of achieving compliance. The team came to realize that regulatory agencies often serve all citizens, thus making all members of the American public potential customers. For example, any citizen who consumes clean air and safe food uses the services of the Environmental Protection Agency or the Food and Drug Administration. The team then searched for different agency approaches to common regulatory problems, looking for such indicators of regulatory culture change as quality of work-life initiatives, analytical tools, and how the agencies identified and met the needs of employees. The team selected a cross section of safety, commercial, and environmental agencies to represent a broad range of regulatory missions, sizes, and conventions. Following a review of current research in performance, customer service, and management principles, the team identified issues unique to regulatory agencies that are not found in other agencies because regulatory agencies have both "compulsory" and "voluntary" customers.

Compliance of these compulsory customers *can* be gained voluntarily. Industries can work with regulators, whether formally or informally, to improve compliance. Health professionals, academicians, and other professionals often recognize the benefit in the regulator's products and efforts, whether these benefits are protecting public health, enforcing professional standards, or achieving any other outcomes for the public good that judicious regulation can provide.

However distinct the issues may seem to regulatory and enforcement organizations, the solutions are not always unique. Solutions found by other agencies, such as using the Internet to gather opinions, or using focus groups, can help any organization identify issues important to the customer, client, or stakeholder.

Defining your customers and stakeholders begins with where the people are now, not where the organization wants to end up. An organization needs to ask: Who are our customers, and why are they important? What are the needs of each group? What do they look for, and how do we know that? What are our customers' current problems? How will each goal benefit them? One recommendation is to divide both customers and stakeholders by their roles in the process: as doers, supporters, or influencers.

Manager Alert

Defining your customers and stakeholders begins with where the people are now, not where the organization wants to end up.

BEST PRACTICES

Best practices in use among public-sector organizations, identified by the National Partnership for Reinventing Government and the National Academy of Public Administration, include

- Use an integrated, intranet-based, management information system to capture, disseminate, and monitor performance and data.
- Establish employee and external customer research capabilities and causal baseline and trend information.

- Implement organizational improvements based on employee and customer data.
- Tie performance and budget requests and justifications to Congress based on performance information.
- Where possible, combine reports of performance to the public and Congress. (In some organizations, reports to Congress may be classified.)
- Link mission success via customer and employee surveys to establish a connection.
- Simplify. Some organizations have dramatically streamlined the performance measurement process, tracking fewer but higher-quality indicators. Their strategic and business plans are short, easy-to-read documents.
- Integrate strategic planning with budget.
- Create supportive leadership through involvement and sign off on requirements.
- Develop a customer-focused strategic plan and performance measures.
- Align strategic goals with budgets.
- Involve external stakeholders in extensive reviews of goals and measures.

Chapter 3

ORGANIZING YOUR CONSULTATION PROCESS: ASSESSING CURRENT REALITY AND PLANNING FOR THE FUTURE

The consultation process, working with your customers, stakeholders and partners, should be ongoing through the entire development of the strategic plan. This should include formulation of the mission statement, development of goals, and agreement on the final product (to the extent possible). Focus groups, workshops, and retreats are a good way to bring people together away from the daily workplace. Being off-site helps people to focus on the task at hand.

Even strategic planning requires planning! In developing your goals and objectives and in continuing to monitor the degree of success you achieve, you need to determine how you want to gather feedback from all those affected by your organization. A well-developed plan of action is critical to the success of any organization, providing a road map of where your organization wants to go and the route it will take to get there.

Manager Alert
Planning requires imagination, creativity, and fortitude. Things never go smoothly, so be prepared!

THE STRATEGIC PLANNING PROCESS

Formal strategic planning asks and then answers important questions in an orderly way, creating a scale of priority and urgency. The process introduces a new set of decision-making forces and tools. It requires management to look at the organization as an integrated whole rather than to plan separately for each component of the business. It forces the setting of objectives for such things as achievement of mission. Future opportunities and threats are clarified. Through the experience, knowledge, and intuition of managers, combined with the systematic collection and evaluation of data, there is a sharper focus on what lies ahead for the organization.

Although most government managers have had some experience with strategic planning, a basic mapping of the process is nevertheless useful for the reader. Figure 3-1 shows the performance measurement process map created by a National Partnership for Reinventing Government benchmarking study. According to this map, there are seven basic phases to strategic planning:

1. Define the basic functions of the organization.
2. Consult with customers, employees, and stakeholders through focus groups, workshops, retreats, and so on, focusing on the following:
   o   External and internal environmental assessment
   o   SWOT (strengths, weaknesses, opportunities, threats) assessment
   o   Brainstorming
3. Evaluate the potential impact of ideas generated through consultation on each strength, weakness, opportunity, and threat.
4. Create a mission, goals, objectives, and strategies.
5. Analyze the impact of proposed goals, objectives, and strategies on the organization's ability to achieve its basic functions (as identified in Step 1).
6. Finalize and implement strategies, goals, and objectives.
7. Analyze the impact of the organizational functions' actual performance achievement.

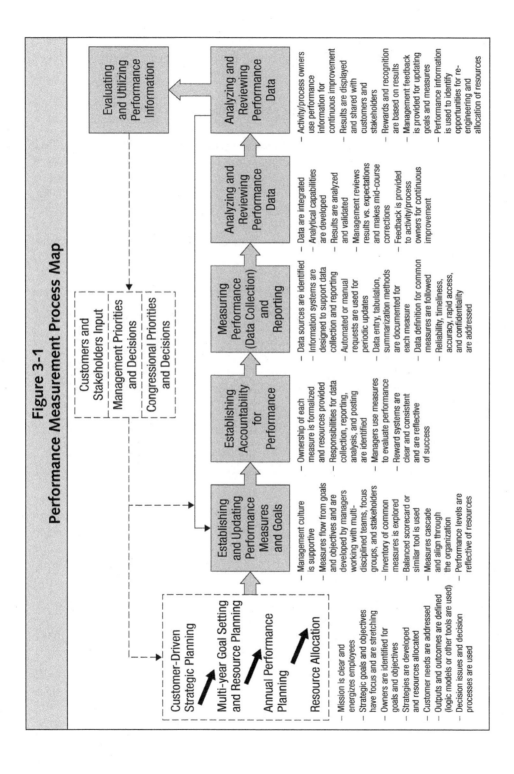

Figure 3-1
Performance Measurement Process Map

By linking decision-making with basic organizational functions, an organization creates a framework for making complex, politically sensitive decisions at all levels of the process and at all levels of the organization.

TERMS USED IN STRATEGIC PLANNING

Strategic planning is a long-term, future-oriented process of assessment, goal setting, and decision-making that (1) maps an explicit path between the present and a vision of the future, (2) relies on careful consideration of an organization's capabilities and environment, and (3) leads to priority-based resource allocation and other decisions. A well-organized strategic planning system aligns long-range visions, such as mission statements, with the essential levels of short-range functional targets. The results are better teamwork, job efficiency, financial control, and visible performance measures.

Manager Alert

Here are some tips for managers:

- Create long-range plans for organizational growth or change.
- Use an integrated approach that not only encompasses short- and long-range goals but also recognizes the requirements of day-to-day operations.
- Make the most of limited fiscal resources by not limiting yourself to doing what was done before.
- Look at alternative methods to implement the planning process.

Strategies are methods to achieve goals and objectives. They align the organization with the environment in which it must function. Formulated from goals and objectives, a strategy is the means for transforming inputs into outputs, and ultimately outcomes, with the best use of resources. A strategy reflects budgetary and other resources.

A *vision* is a description of a preferred future. Not bound by time, a vision represents global and continuing purposes and serves as a foundation for a system of strategic planning. A vision depicts an ideal future and the contributions that a public-sector organization can make to that end.

It is difficult to determine where you want your organization to be in 10, 20, or 30 years. However, having a vision of the future is what strategic planning is all about. An important element of successful strategizing is to understand the difference between what should never change and what should be open for change.

Mission is the reason for an organization's existence. It succinctly identifies what the organization does, why it does it, and for whom. A mission statement reminds everyone—the public, legislators, courts, and agency personnel—of the unique purposes promoted and served by the organization.

Goals are major milestones, usually at the program level. They are the general ends toward which efforts are directed. Goals address issues by stating policy intention. They are both qualitative and quantifiable, but not quantified. In a strategic planning system, they are ranked for priority. Goals stretch and challenge, but they are realistic and achievable.

A goal should need little or no explanation. It should provide inspiration to employees and be tangible—that is, everyone should know when the goal has been achieved. There are some excellent examples to be found in history:

- Put a man on the moon by the end of the decade and return him safely (Kennedy 1961)

- Become the dominant player in commercial aircraft and bring the world into the jet age (Boeing 1950)

- Crush Adidas (Nike 1960s) and Destroy Yamaha (Honda 1970s).

Manager Alert

A goal should need little or no explanation. It should provide inspiration to employees and be tangible.

External/internal assessment is an evaluation of key factors that influence an organization's success in achieving its mission and goals. Detailed evaluation of trends, conditions, opportunities, and obstacles directs the development of each element of the strategic plan. Key external factors may include economic conditions, population shifts, technological advances, geographical changes, and statutory changes. Key internal factors include management policies, resource constraints, organizational structure, automation, personnel, and operational procedures.

Objectives are planned activities that are measurable and time-sensitive (usually one-year or two-year) and that keep the organization moving toward achievement of its mission, as defined through its basic functions. Objectives are clear targets for specific action. They mark interim steps toward achieving a long-range mission and goals. Linked directly to goals, objectives are measurable, time-based statements of intent that emphasize the results of actions at the end of a specific time.

Outcome measures are indicators of the actual impact upon a stated condition or problem. They are tools to assess the effectiveness of organizational performance, public performance, and public benefit derived. An outcome measure is typically expressed as a percentage, rate, or ratio.

Do not discount past planning activities, even if they predate current activities. For example, if a Total Quality Management (TQM) analysis was performed on the annual budget process, there may already be a defined set of key performance indicators. Alternatively, an environmental analysis may have been conducted during a program review or evaluation. All of these can be included in the process without reinventing the wheel.

The basic functions of the organization (step 1 above) anchor organizational decisions. The methodology is designed to help decisionmakers explore and understand the relationships between the organization, the objectives it seeks to achieve, and the environment. Alignment results from analysis of feedback and consultation, including a SWOT assessment (see below). Brainstorming should focus on generating ideas that make strengths stronger and weaknesses weaker, take advantage of opportunities, and neutralize threats.

Ideas generated through consultation should be evaluated in terms of their impact on the organization's ability to achieve its mission. Any form of consultation should be designed to foster communication, analysis, and insight into the organization's daily operations. Those consulted, whether customers, clients, stakeholders, or employees, should understand the plan and their role in its development and implementation.

Manager Alert

A manager interested in balancing the strategic process should find a workable, practical way to achieve the desired results while making the most of decreasing resources—both human and monetary.

If management works closely with the employee, they can create a work environment in which all are involved and clearly understand their roles in achieving the organization's mission. If individual targets coordinate performance with the mission of the organization, then project leaders, first-line supervisors, mid-managers, and functional executives always know where they fit into the overall plan. As a result, performance evaluation becomes a positive work-focusing activity instead of a stressful "report card."

A balanced approach to strategic planning also improves motivation and morale. If employees have a role in the creation of their own destiny and know what is expected of them, they have a sense of accomplishment when it is achieved.

Increased, open communication with the customer and stakeholder will have a positive effect on their satisfaction with the organization's performance.

FORMULATING THE MISSION STATEMENT

A mission statement captures the essence of why the organization exists and should be a brief statement of organizational purpose. This is an important first step in the strategic planning process.

To create a mission statement, the participants should consider the question "What is the organization's reason for existence?" The facilitator will probably want to "board" the ideas as they are generated.

Boarding is a method in which each participant is given either a small pad of paper (such as 3"× 3" Post-Its) or index cards on which to write down their ideas. Each participant records one idea in three to eight words on each card. The facilitator then collects the cards and groups them by common theme, thus finding the vital few most important ideas.

When this is completed, the facilitator reviews each idea and asks if the concept is actually something for which the organization is responsible or if it is a part of the process toward achievement of the mission. One to five ideas should evolve. They should then be merged into as brief a statement as possible: the mission statement.

Mission statements are created for both internal and external use. Internally, they provide direction and should reflect the organizational vision. Externally, mission statements inform and contribute to an organization's public image. However, if an organization tries to please everyone, it will please no one. The resultant mission statement will merely state what the organization has in common with other similar organizations, rather than describing its uniqueness.

Establishing goals, objectives, and strategies forms the basis for your strategic plan. While there is no single strategic planning system that works in all circumstances, the process will include determining the mission of your organization; developing a profile of your organization that reflects its internal conditions and capabilities; assessing your organization's external environment; analyzing options that match your organization's profile with its external environment while keeping in mind its mission; choosing longer term objectives and the strategies to achieve them; developing annual objectives and shorter-term strategies compatible with the longer-term objectives and strategies; implementing strategic choices that match the people, tasks, resources, and reward systems; and periodic review and evaluation.

The size and nature of your organization will dictate the formality of the planning process. A large organization with diversified operations requires a more formal process than a smaller organization whose operations are less complex. Strategic planning is, however, a creative process. If management decides in isolation what the goals and objectives will be and merely asks the next level of management to provide some numbers, the resulting document will be useless and irrelevant. The current reality and organizational culture of each entity is unique, as is its societal role and impact.

Consequently, each strategic plan must be unique and reflect extensive consultation. A balanced approach to consultation and planning is the means to an end. If done correctly, it will result in high performance, good customer service, and trust in the capabilities of the organization, both internally and externally.

Manager Alert

A balanced approach to consultation and planning will result in high performance, good customer service, and trust in the capabilities of the organization, both internally and externally.

One successful method for conducting consultation is to gather individuals together for discussion, selecting them according to their area of interest. For example, an organization such as the Federal Emergency Management Agency (FEMA), which works closely with state and local governments, would gather a group of state and local representatives. This group would be separate and apart from federal partners FEMA would work with during a disaster. After the discussion, be prepared to evaluate and analyze input and report back on the impact of the group's consultation with you. This type of consultation is usually referred to as a focus group.

FOCUS GROUPS

A focus group, as defined by the Federal Highway Administration within the Department of Transportation, is a small selected number of individuals who meet to discuss a single topic. Focus groups serve as a tool for gathering opinions and perspectives and should have the following features: a limited agenda (no more than five or six major questions); no more than 15 people; structured to gather insights and opinions through conversation and interaction; and minimal presentation of material to set context and subject. The Bureau of Land Management also uses focus groups in its strategic planning consultation process.

The informal environment established by a focus group encourages participation. The small size lowers barriers, allowing people to speak out without fear of criticism. Focus groups are not, however, appropriate to all situations. They serve a narrowly defined need for direct and informal opinion on a specific topic. Their special uses include obtaining community input from individuals not otherwise represented, gathering expert opinion on a plan, and comparing opinions on a concept (e.g., an internal and an external focus group). Information from a focus group should supplement other forms of consultation.

Using Focus Groups

Organizing your customers, stakeholders, and employees into focus groups will permit those interested in common issues to provide their feedback at the same time. Focus groups will also help the government manager coordinate responses so that possibly opposing viewpoints may be discussed in the same meeting.

Focus groups should use a facilitator, who is essential to hold the group to the agenda and ensure that each participant has an opportunity to speak. The organization conducting the focus group needs to provide guidance to the facilitator regarding the agenda and purpose of the focus group.

A focus group meeting should not exceed two hours and should be scheduled to meet the specific needs of the selected participants. For example, if the organization wants the opinion of working individuals, the meeting should be scheduled for non-work hours, both to encourage participation and to minimize inconvenience to the participants.

On the downside, a focus group only gives you qualitative responses and is not statistically representative of the entire population. It does not meet federal standards for continuing public involvement and cannot replace the more formal process of recording comments and presenting them to appropriate authorities.

A focus group is a discussion carefully planned and used to obtain ideas and opinions on a limited area of interest in a nonthreatening environment. A facilitator is usually used, and participation is usually kept to a small number of people. Discussions should be comfortable for participants and encourage them to share their perceptions.

A focus group meeting is a structured process conducted for the purpose of obtaining detailed information about a particular topic or issue. Focus group discussions are particularly useful in the early stages of planning when the precise issues that would permit a more specific research technique (such as a sample survey) may not be known. These types of discussions are also useful both to gather data and to lay the groundwork for more precise evaluation methods.

What a Focus Group Will (and Won't) Accomplish

Focus groups are relatively easy to undertake. They are a good way to "interview" a number of people simultaneously, and results can be obtained in a short time span. The interaction provides freer responses, reflecting the interactive and spontaneous nature of the session. Participants will usually express views that they might not express in other settings, such as when they are interviewed individually.

Including a facilitator is usually advisable. Guidance should be provided to the facilitator to ensure clarification or greater detail on specific issues of interest to your organization. However, keep in mind that unanticipated lines of discussion may also prove of use to final analysis. Focus groups can work well not only with a specific population, but also with a diverse one. People who may normally be reticent about expressing personal views often do well in this type of environment.

The facilitator's capabilities will make a big difference. The facilitator must be able to manage the group discussion while encouraging free expression and a steady flow of ideas. Scheduling can also be an issue. It is sometimes difficult to get all the players in the same location at the same time.

Playing Politics

Another factor that is specific to the public sector can be a very difficult one for management to handle. Sometimes an individual or group of individuals may be reticent to express an opinion in front of representatives of the organization for fear of appearing to not be "team players." They may believe that, if they appear too critical, they will lose their access to the organization's leadership, rendering them ineffectual. Consultation is valuable only as long as the opinions received are honest and open. Reassuring the participants will not address the issue; it is similar to the old joke "we are from the government and we're here to help." (Notice that you still chuckle when you read that, even now.)

There are a number of ways to handle this issue. One way is not to have any organizational representatives at the focus group meeting. If this route is chosen, be sure that the facilitator is completely prepared for the meeting, knows exactly what the priorities are, and yet can be on the lookout for emerging relevant issues.

Another possibility is to provide self-addressed large envelopes with surveys of specific issues of interest to the organization, allowing for anonymous submissions. If this is done, be sure the participants know the time frame in which they must submit their observations.

Analysis and Evaluation

Evaluating the results of the meeting also presents many challenges. It must be remembered that the individual responses were influenced by ongoing discussions and not independently made. Quite a lot of specific information can be generated, making analysis difficult. Also remember that the participants were not randomly chosen, but rather selected based on their interests (and possibly their availability), so do not freely generalize the findings and conclusions.

Defining Participation in a Focus Group

First, ask what the session should produce. Identify the issues for which data should be collected. Once identified, organize the participants, whether employees, customers, stakeholders, or any combination thereof, according to their areas of interest.

Groups should represent specific segments of the population that have an interest in a particular issue. Conditions should promote both comfort and independence of thought, to maximize discussion and self-disclosure. Focus groups should have around 12 members (not counting the facilitator and someone to keep notes). Smaller groups tend to be dominated by one or two people, and larger groups can inhibit participation by all members. A group of around 12 people will usually provide both a variety of ideas and interactive participation.

Manager Alert
Focus groups should represent specific segments of the population that have an interest in a particular issue.

Conducting the Session

No focus group session should last more than two hours because after that a discussion will begin to lose momentum. The goal is to get as much information on the table as possible. Open discussion should always be encouraged. Group interaction can bring out additional information. The facilitator should stimulate the discussion and keep it on course. Every response and observation should be considered valid. The exercise should be viewed as a gathering of information, with neither support nor criticism of any comment. A session facilitator should not try to resolve an issue, address an individual problem or concern, or reach a conclusion.

Summary

Although the presentation of findings will vary somewhat depending on the objectives of the evaluation and the nature of the findings, it is generally useful to present both quantitative and qualitative results. Quantitative results—such as the number of statements that comment on outcomes of asset accumulation or the proportion of comments that are favorable or unfavorable—provide summary information.

Qualitative results can be obtained by using representative comments from focus group participants to create a clearer image of participants' viewpoints. In most cases, the findings will simply report the views of focus group participants as they have expressed them. The strength of a focus group method is that issues can clearly be seen from the participants' perspectives. Comments should meet the following two simple criteria: (1) each is clearly and directly related to the subject discussed; and (2) each makes a consistent point. Comments should be organized to illustrate main themes. Background information and interpretation of findings should be integrated into the report only as appropriate.

WORKSHOPS/RETREATS

Most will agree that strategic planning is vital to a public-sector organization's success. A focus group is only one of many techniques that allow a group of people to share opinions and contribute to the development of a strategic plan. A workshop or retreat, usually reserved for internal consultations, is another method of consultation.

As with focus groups, the role of the workshop facilitator is a critical one. There are no right or wrong answers. The most successful workshops allow the participants to explore unlimited options and then select those that best apply to the organization.

The following elements are recommended for a successful workshop:

- There should be a keynote speaker to walk everyone through the overall process and set the tone.
- The workshop should last at least one day, but never more than three.
- Designate a workshop "architect" who will interact with the executive team, helping them to develop and implement a strategic planning framework.
- Designate someone to assess the effectiveness of the current strategic plan, as well as any current processes. (This is usually someone external to the organization, who can provide an objective viewpoint.)
- Designate a workshop "coach" who can work with teams to develop and implement strategic planning across all levels of the organization.
- Bring in a professional to design the workshop and serve as facilitator for any planning sessions.

BRAINSTORMING

Brainstorming is a creative facilitation tool that works best with large groups. It is a method that uses combined skills and intelligence. A brainstorming group should concentrate on a specific issue. For the process to work effectively, it is important that the "rules" of brainstorming be followed. It is the facilitator's responsibility to ensure that the process moves smoothly.

> ## Manager Alert
> A brainstorming group should concentrate on a specific issue.

The Rules of Brainstorming

There are no "wrong" ideas. Even if an idea seems silly, it may trigger another, more useful, idea in others:

- Do not criticize ideas, either verbally or with body language.
- Build on each other's ideas. Be creative!
- Generate as many ideas as possible within the time provided.
- Record all ideas. No one, not even the facilitator, should decide "worthiness."
- Periods of silence are okay—let ideas simmer.

The concept of the "vital few," a product of the quality revolution in the United States, was popularized by Joseph Juran, PhD, who drew upon the work of Alfredo Pareto, an Italian economist. The principle of the vital few is that 80 percent of the problems experienced in a process can be accounted for by 20 percent of the core causes. Therefore, if one attacks and resolves or eliminates these "vital few" causes, 80 percent of the problems can be solved.

In strategic planning, there are initially many ideas when a group is determining the strengths of the organization. From that list, 20 percent are selected as the most important. These primary, vital strengths are those that represent 80 percent of the assets of the organization, and thus it is these few strengths that are considered in the strategic planning process. One way to determine the vital few is to ask the group the following question: "If you could count on only X number of strengths to aid the organization in the future, which ones would you choose?"

As you create an organizational vision, there are some basic questions to be asked:

- What should this organization look like in 5, 10, 20, and 30 years?
- How should our employees and customers feel about us?
- What should the organization achieve?
- If there is a piece in the newspaper or a magazine discussing our organization, what would we want it to say?

The final steps in the above process are integrating the vision statement and the analysis, and then identifying the strategic actions that will allow the organization to realize the vision.

SWOT ASSESSMENTS

A SWOT (strengths, weaknesses, opportunities, threats) assessment views the strengths and weaknesses inherent in an organization and the opportunities and threats that the organization may face. Arising from a variety of trends, strengths and weaknesses are assets and liabilities that are internal to the organization and over which the organization should have control. Opportunities and threats are conditions that tend to be external to the organization and are generally not under the organization's direct control.

Making the SWOT assessment consists of the following steps: defining the business; identifying core competencies, critical success factors, opportunities, threats, strengths, and weaknesses; and assessing current strategies. The following steps summarize the process:

- Brainstorm all of the issues with which the organization must cope or things it might do in the time frame of the plan. The vision, assumptions, strengths, weaknesses, opportunities, and threats affecting the organization must be clearly defined in order for the brainstorming to have optimal value.

- Discuss and classify each issue as either an end result or an action to reach an end result.

- Integrate all actions into a coherent and meaningful set of strategies. Many of the items will be subsets or tactics of a larger strategic thrust.

- Integrate the results into meaningful groups. These are the objectives of the organization.

- Prioritize the objectives. Then prioritize the strategies on the basis of the priority of the objectives, and identify what any one strategy will contribute to the accomplishment of any one objective.

At this point, you have the full framework of a strategic plan. The details within strategies are the measures with time frames and identified individual responsibilities for execution.

The SWOT assessment, which can be done either by a focus group or in a workshop, is an effective way to assess the current reality for an organization. The analysis itself, using the SWOT framework, will frequently be sufficient to reveal the types of changes that are necessary to the success of goals and objectives. The following types of questions should be addressed when conducting a SWOT assessment. Each participant in the discussion should write down individual answers, and then the facilitator can "board" them for discussion. (For an explanation of "boarding," see the previous section on brainstorming.)

To determine the strengths, decide: (1) What advantages does the organization have over others that may have similar societal roles? (2) Which things are done particularly well? In answering these questions, determine the answers from the organization's point of view and from the point of view of the client (remember, *client* includes both the customer and the taxpayer). Don't be modest, but be realistic.

To determine the weaknesses, determine: (1) What things are not done well by the organization? (2) What improvements could be made? (3) Is there anything that should be avoided? As with strengths, think about these questions from both points of view. Sometimes there is a perceived weakness that will make an impact on the organization, even if it doesn't really exist. It is especially important to be realistic about weaknesses and deal with them openly.

Opportunities are determined through the following questions: (1) Where are the organization's best chances for success? (2) Are there new trends or technologies that can help the organization improve its operations? (3) Is there training readily available in these technologies for the employee? (4) Are there recent changes in government (federal, state, or other) policy that have had a positive impact on the daily operations? Societal attitudes, among other things, can also provide opportunities for an organization.

Threats are determined by looking at the obstacles to success. For the private sector, the consideration of competition is vital. In the public sector, this is not the case. Threats to the public sector include such things as societal attitude and politics. Is there a member of Congress (or state legislature) who wants to reduce your funding or perhaps eliminate your organization completely? Are the types of service or benefits the organization provides being redefined or now considered unnecessary by the taxpayer? Do changes in technology affect how the organization does its job?

Carrying out a SWOT assessment not only reveals what needs to be done but also puts into perspective the issues and problems facing an organization.

A WORD ABOUT PUTTING IT ALL TOGETHER

All the successful organizations cited within this book not only include the customers, stakeholders, and employees in their planning activities but also report back to them through both published reports and the Internet. The importance of communication is discussed at length in Chapter 5.

General Electric CEO Jack Welch once said, "The winners . . . will be those who can develop a culture that allows them to move faster, communicate more clearly, and involve everyone in a focused effort to serve ever more demanding customers." This is as true for the public sector as it is for the private.

All three elements—customer/stakeholder, employee, and mission achievement—need to be integrated. This can be done either incrementally or all at once. For example, an organization may start with the management process, analyzing and improving the internal organization first, then move to joint accountability and team evaluations. When that is complete, the organization can move outward, involving customers and stakeholders. Other organizations find that consulting with the customer and stakeholder first helps focus the employee discussions.

However the changes are made and whatever the process is called, to be effective, long-term change and improvement must integrate all of the key areas. Only through a balanced approach to customer service, performance and process management, and employee involvement can organizations become leaders in their fields.

Consultation, whether through focus groups or other methods, should be designed to glean the opinions and expectations of those affected by an organization's activities. Form a partnership with customers, stakeholders, and employees—don't control them. The more an organization forms partnerships with those who have a vested interest in the success of the organization, the more successful that organization is likely to be. Some of the most successful organizations work closely not only with customers and employees, but also with unions and legislators. Better communication results in an increased level of trust.

CORE VALUES

Core values reflect the individuals within the organization, especially the values of the leaders of the organization. To define your organization's core values, discuss the following questions in a meeting setting or a workshop:

- What core values do you bring to work? These are values that are so basic that you would practice them whether or not they were rewarded.
- What core values do you hope your children will hold when they go to work?
- Do you believe that these values are so basic that they would be valid in any circumstances?
- What would happen to these values if they interfered with achievement of the organization's mission?
- Which values would be basic to every organization, everywhere?

Try to set individual performance targets that align with the strategic direction of the organization. If you do that, individual employees, project leaders, first-line supervisors, and midlevel and senior managers will always know where they fit into the overall plan. As a result of that process, individual and team performance evaluation can become a positive factor, focusing on future activity instead of on a stressful "report card."

Manager Alert

Try to set individual performance targets that align with the strategic direction of the organization.

Chapter 4

CONSULTATION AT ITS BEST: INVOLVING EVERYONE IN AN ITERATIVE PROCESS

The goal of the federal manager is not to control customers, stakeholders, and employees, but to form partnerships with them. The more you partner with those who have a vested interest in the success of the organization, the more successful that organization is likely to be. Some of the most successful organizations work closely not only with customers and employees but also with unions and legislators. Better communication results in an increased level of trust.

Successful public-sector organizations will

- Communicate regularly with employees, customers, and stakeholders
- Use self-assessment tools, such as the Baldrige criteria (published by the Baldrige Performance Excellence Program, National Institute of Standards and Technology; www.nist.gov/baldrige/about/index.cfm)
- Involve the legislative branch through consultation or representation on working groups and committees
- Involve the customer, stakeholder, and employee at every phase of the management process
- Involve the unions early and often.

A strategy is a shared understanding about how a goal is to be reached, and a balanced approach allows management to communicate that strategy clearly to customers and employees. Objectives translate into a system of performance measurements that communicates a powerful, forward-looking, strategic focus to everyone. That line of communication begins with well-organized consultation.

LISTENING TO YOUR CUSTOMERS AND STAKEHOLDERS

Once an organization has opened the doors to communication with customers and stakeholders regarding performance management, it is vital that it maintain the flow of information. The customer who has been involved in the planning process will want to know how things are going. The more informed the stakeholders are, the more feedback an organization will receive in the next round of planning—and the better that planning will be as a result.

No matter how many focus groups or other types of consultation sessions are held, they will never include the views of everyone. The individual on the street can sometimes provide that one idea that had been missing all along. Don't discount that viewpoint.

Realize that not everyone is on the Internet. This is especially important for headquarters personnel; there is a mentality, especially in the federal sector, that assumes that everyone is online. Those who work in the field offices generally know that if you want to reach the man or woman on the street, you need to use other media as well.

Public support will also be created because the customer has been allowed input into what is needed and how best to deliver it. The customer is also the client and a constituent, and the importance of customer support should never be underestimated.

Manager Alert
Never underestimate the importance of customer support.

The public-sector organization today is as much a customer-driven organization as a private-sector corporation is. The federal sector particularly is striving to create a customer-driven government that works better and costs less. Public-sector organizations must demonstrate success in meeting program goals and outcomes. This is a major challenge to today's manager: the need to balance the demand for program improvements with decreasing resource availability. The budget process in the public sector especially is driven by performance, and marginal dollars are given to programs that achieve their stated goals.

How a customer perceives the organization's performance has become a priority for some public-sector organizations. Customer service measures should reflect the factors that are of real concern to the customer.

The Internet is transforming the way public-sector organizations and customers interact. The catalysts in many cases are the independent technology consultants who create software programs. These programs provide both the public sector and the customer with the ability to communicate. The public-sector organization puts its draft documents on the Internet, and the customer (and stakeholder and employee) can review the documents and provide feedback. This also allows for open communication throughout the year, not just at the time of a special meeting.

In developing its strategic framework, a public-sector organization should make maximum use of all available communication tools. The strategic framework (see Chapter 7) must address customer service, ensuring that the business strategy is cohesive and customer focused.

The strategy should be developed within the context of the wider strategy of the organization, responsive to the demands of the customer, client, and stakeholder. It should then be implemented as part of the daily operations of the organization and used to monitor its effectiveness and efficiency.

CONSULTING WITH LEGISLATIVE BODIES

Externally, support may be gleaned from the legislative branch, especially if they are partners in the process.

Consultation with the legislative branch is often overlooked as part of the process. Keep in mind that a well-informed legislator is able to be more supportive of a proposed initiative when he or she can explain the mission, objectives, and goals that relate to that initiative.

LISTENING TO YOUR EMPLOYEES

Employees have historical knowledge and experience at the daily operations level. Don't underestimate the importance of this information and expertise. Keep in mind that establishing communication is not an overnight process. Simply saying you are going to work with the employee with whatever phrase you choose—consult with, empower, enable, team build with—does not just happen magically. For example, the term *empowerment* has become virtually meaningless in the public sector.

Building employee trust is more easily said than done, as most public-sector employees have many years' experience with the management idea *du jour*. Introduce and explain the goals of the consultation, making clear that there is a commitment on the part of organizational leadership to make this succeed. Be willing to discuss the commitment to "make it happen" on the part of management and to integrate it into daily operations. Accountability and responsibility need to cascade clearly throughout the organization. Establish an evaluation process based on the performance of both individuals *and* teams relating to stated goals and objectives. Use the performance information gathered to begin the next phase of strategic planning.

When a manager states a desire to *empower* employees and *reengineer* operations to implement some innovative idea, most public-sector employees (especially those who have been in public service for a number of years) will view it as the management theory *du jour* and believe that if they pay lip service to it and keep their heads down, eventually it will go away.

The overuse and misuse of different management tools have rendered them meaningless to the employee. When management talks about building a team, it can mean changing the attitudes of employees or using a team or teams to address some issue or issues. On the other hand, it can also mean filling the organization with employee improvement teams or self-directed work teams with no direct supervision. Reengineering can mean anything from a new management information system to radical changes in the daily processes of the organization, including relationships among employees and customers.

The fact remains that truly involved employees will produce better quality service and higher productivity and be willing to try new things. Most efforts of this type fail because they do not establish the correct groundwork before heading at warp speed to *empower* their employees.

Manager Alert

Truly involved employees will produce better quality service and higher productivity and be willing to try new things.

By no means should you confuse empowerment with programs that are supposed to excite employees through an approach not unlike a pep rally, telling them how to do their jobs by things like "we're a team, let's do it right." This approach only shows the employee how little management knows about the causes of poor performance. Research shows that most service, quality, or productivity problems originate in the structure and processes of the overall organization, not in the activities of the individual.

Creating an involved, empowered workforce takes a lot of work. You need to develop the leadership skills of all levels of management. Training is the key to developing a culture that encourages and supports employee involvement. If employees hear top management asking for their opinion but find their immediate supervisors still behaving as if they have absolute authority, there is little chance of a change in attitude on the part of the individual employee.

Training the employee is also important because poorly trained work teams will hinder rather than help, and processes will be either significantly delayed or full of mistakes.

Management expert Peter Drucker says, "So much of what we call management consists of making it difficult for people to work." Managers can empower employees until the cows come home, but if the employees are not able to make a difference, they see empowerment as a way of placing the blame on them for the failure of management.

Employees must have analytical skills to evaluate the processes they use and clarify what is expected of them, both by their managers and by customers. To do this, they need training in how to use problem-solving tools and techniques. In determining their expectations, they should know from senior management what improvements or areas of attention are the most important to the organization.

Senior management needs to support training and sharing of information with the employees and be willing to help eliminate any barriers that may be created by the existing culture of the organization. The need for strong leadership is discussed at length in Chapter 6.

The organization needs to help its employees learn how to communicate with stakeholders and customers, both internal and external. Employees need to understand how perceptions influence communication and responses. And they need the analytical tools to identify ways to create mutually beneficial relationships and build rapport with others. These tools are vital if the employee is to represent the organization well.

Manager Alert

The organization needs to help its employees learn how to communicate with stakeholders and customers, both internal and external.

Information technology makes it possible to keep all employees, both at headquarters and in the field, equally informed about performance data. Most of our research partners use a combination of the intranet, Internet, and e-mail to keep their employees informed and current on organizational performance. Many also use newsletters and hard-copy postings to communicate this information to employees. Our more successful partners make a concerted effort to ensure constant communication with employees. Best practices include using the intranet and Internet for regular information and using supplementary and complementary dissemination mechanisms to ensure delivery of the message. Not everyone has access to the web, and any communication strategy should keep that in mind.

PARTNERING WITH UNIONS

There's an old saying: If you are not part of the solution, you are part of the problem. Unions can fall into either category, but partnership with unions is especially critical in achieving culture change within an organization.

BEST PRACTICES/ENABLERS

Following are some best practices gleaned from successful planning organizations:

- **True leadership by the executives.** Participation by the executive staff in the development of the performance measures for which they will be accountable helps to create ownership. They must be clear about expectations and true champions of the performance objectives they sponsor. However, this is an iterative process of change.
- **Quarterly executive management meetings.** Quarterly meetings at which managements reports on objectives are an effective mechanism to support accountability for performance.
- **A planning guidance document**. Develop an annual guidebook that describes an overview of the planning framework and guides the development and management of agency plans. It will provide a consistent process for staff to follow and reduce the learning curve. The planning guide will also help drive strategic management throughout the agency.
- **Continuing knowledge development.** Continue to train and orient employees at all levels on the strategic planning process. Training and technical support should be continually provided to professional staff involved in performance management. The agency also distributes the annual performance plan (to all who work at the headquarters and to all managers) and the Strategic Plan as a reference tool for day-to-day work.
- **Customer focus.** This is the underpinning of agency planning.
- **Budget and planning postmortems.** These identify planning and budget process improvements for the next planning cycle, whether every year, every three years, or every five years.

LESSONS LEARNED

Change is hard, but the more you involve and communicate, the more quickly change occurs.

Executives are busy with near-term management. It is important to make the strategic management process as painless as possible so they can also effectively focus on the long term, for which staff involvement and support are key.

Because the program experts in the area you are measuring will be held accountable, they need to be involved. Champions—high-level executives who visibly support a program—and process owners are an integral part of the planning process. For performance measures to be used to manage, they must tie in to systems and budgeted resource allocation.

Chapter 5

THE NEED TO COMMUNICATE

Comedian Jackie "Moms" Mabley once said: "If you always do what you always did, then you'll always get what you always got." Even assuming that you do a tremendous job of formulating your plans and setting and achieving your stated goals, you will still need to communicate that success (and any failures) to your customers, stakeholders, and employees. Otherwise, you will "get what you always got"—a feeling of isolation, secrecy, and mistrust from both the customer and the employee.

Part of the strategic planning process should be a clearly defined communications strategy that is dynamic, frequent, and reflective of the needs of both management and audience. The communications strategy will be used at all phases of the process, initially for consultation in the development of mission, goals, and objectives. After performance information has been gathered and evaluated, the strategy should work to communicate the successes and failures of the organization. Next is another cycle of consultation to improve the process. Then it begins again! With each performance and planning cycle, the strategy becomes more finely honed to serve each audience well, building an environment of honesty and openness.

DEVELOPING A COMMUNICATIONS STRATEGY

Communication is a driver of organizational excellence, where failure is as easy to discuss as success. The principal function of a communications strategy is to get the right information to the right people at the right time to help them make informed decisions regarding the organization's activities (Table 5-1).

Table 5-1 Planning a Communications Strategy	
Poor Communications	Good Communications
Management "knows best"	Everyone is aware of changing needs
Performance measures are focused on internal controls	Performance measures are based in perceptions of value—to the customer, stakeholder, and employee
Individual units are "stovepiped," with a narrow view of their individual functions; the mission of the organization is secondary	Managers understand how the activities of their individual units affect the achievement of the organizational mission
The role of employees is to serve the organization	The role of employees is to serve customers, be responsible to stakeholders, and partner with each other to achieve the mission of the organization
Resource allocation and budget decisions are the sole prerogative of management	Resource allocation and budget decisions are made openly, based on performance data collection and analysis
All information is held close by management and not shared among units within an organization or with the public	Information is shared both internally and externally; limitations are based only on individual privacy or security needs

Manager Alert

The principal function of a communications strategy is to get the right information to the right people at the right time.

A communications strategy should begin with no assumptions. Do not let organizational decisions get mired in an attitude of "been there, done that." Be aware of the fact that, as a manager, you may not even know what you need. Technology is changing at a rapid rate, but new, fancy (not to mention expensive) products and services are not always the most useful. The public-sector manager must trust the judgment of the workforce and common sense instead of relying exclusively on government specifications.

Remember the SWOT (strengths, weaknesses, opportunities, threats) assessment discussed in Chapter 3? What tools are currently available to the organization for communication? Where will the different types of consultation work best (e.g., focus group, surveys)? What will success look like, internally and externally?

The overarching challenge of reinventing government is full-time communication. Because of the federal government's size and complexity, communication in the public sector is a full-time job. Working for the public sector is not just filling in forms; it is the collective action of dedicated individuals. Government reinvention, when done correctly, produces results and promotes open communication.

CHANGING THE MANAGEMENT STYLE THROUGH COMMUNICATION

As an initial step, determine the current organizational culture. Today, successful organizations are doing what was once considered impossible: increasing customer satisfaction, shortening process cycles and response times, reducing costs, and developing innovative new products and services, all at the same time. Not long ago, organizations could succeed by excelling at one or two of these, but the landscape is now littered with the victims of this obsolete thinking. Today's leaders are capitalizing on the changes and challenges facing all organizations by being better, faster, cheaper, and newer than their less nimble competitors.

Transforming a traditional organization to one that's better, faster, cheaper, and newer is extremely difficult. Organizations in both the public and private sectors have built powerful cultures, systems, and practices that may have been pointed in the wrong direction. This is especially true in the public sector, where organizational cultural change must be an integral part of performance management and measurement.

Manager Alert

In the public sector, organizational cultural change must be an integral part of performance management and measurement.

Historically, management cultures have formed around three different styles of decision-making: internally focused, functionally managed, and management centered. Discussions of each style follow.

Internally Focused Management Decisions

Most decisions about products, services, and organizational direction are made from the inside out, so that management decisions are internally focused. Specialists, technical experts, managers, planners, and other professionals spend most of their time inside the organization pushing products and services out to the customer.

Here, the needs of the organization are put ahead of those people it is trying to serve. John McDonnell, Chairman and CEO of McDonnell-Douglas, once said of the organization's past practices, "We did not always listen to what the customer had to say before telling him what he wanted." This "we know best" approach found many corporate leaders out of sync with their customers, stakeholders, and employees. Their bottom line fell significantly, and their customers, treated as a captive audience, found products and services that better reflected their changing perceptions. Similarly, public-sector organizations are now finding that the level of confidence in their product or service has dropped for the same reason: We need to learn to ask customers what they need, not tell them.

Functionally Managed Decisions

Functionally managed organizations typically reduce service and quality levels while increasing cycle times and costs. Some symptoms of this type of management include an "us-versus-them" approach to communications, fighting for organizational resources, unmanaged gaps between departments that disrupt cross-functional work processes, improvements or changes in one department that impede the effectiveness of other departments, and losing sight of the "big picture."

Here, individual departments work to optimize their own internal efficiency. Goals, objectives, measurements, and career paths move up and down within the narrow, functional "stovepipes." Functional managers and their employees focus on doing their own jobs or segments of the production, delivery, or support process.

Management-Centered Decisions

Management's needs, goals, and perspectives are the starting point for all activities. Managers and their staff professionals are the brains, and employees are the hands. Employees serve their managerial masters and do as they are told. Broad business perspectives and strategies, operational performance data, problem-solving and decision-making authority, and cross-functional skills are kept by management.

But the world is now moving too fast to maintain this type of approach, which puts management at the center of planning and coordination. Managers can no longer know enough, fast enough, enough of the time to anticipate enough of the changes that are needed to make the organization better, faster, and more efficient.

Recognizing that organizations sometimes need to reverse direction quickly, many organizations implemented a variety of improvement programs and processes:

- **Employee involvement and empowerment.** Many training and motivational programs, as well as structural changes, aim to move daily problem-solving, decision-making, customer satisfaction, and productivity improvement responsibilities closer to the front lines.

- **Teams.** A rapidly growing employee involvement trend uses departmental, problem-solving, cross-functional, project, process-improvement, planning and coordinating, and self-directed work teams in many combinations and configurations.

- **Customer service.** Increasingly, organizations are identifying key customer groups, clarifying and ranking their expectations, working to realign the organization's systems customer around those expectations, and training employees to deal with customers more effectively.

- **Process improvement and reengineering.** Data-based tools and techniques, flowcharting, and other mapping approaches improve processes at micro- or departmental levels. In other cases, processes are radically reengineered across vertical departments at macro- or strategic levels.

- **Training and development.** Many executives recognize the need for massive improvements in skill levels throughout their organizations. This recognition is leading to increased technical communications and effectiveness, data-based tools and techniques, process improvement and management, and coaching of skill development.

- **Technology.** Investments in automation, information systems, voice and data communication systems, inventory control systems, and so on are growing rapidly as companies push for higher productivity, faster response times, and improved service or quality.

- **Employee involvement.** The organization must align its systems—for reward and recognition, performance management, planning, and information management—to support employee involvement.

- **Using data.** Too often, systems serve accountants, technocrats, or management. Get the cart behind the horse: Systems need to serve either customers or those producing, delivering, or supporting the products or services of the organization.

The basic problem is that people are visible, but the systems and organizational culture by which group and individual behavior is shaped are largely *in*visible. So when something goes wrong, it's easy to trace the problem back to whoever touched it last and lay the blame there.

If you put a good person into a bad system, the system will win. This has been proven so often that it has become a truism in the quality improvement field called the "85/15 Rule." The 85/15 Rule states that if you trace errors or service complaints back to the root cause, about 85 percent of the time the fault lies in the system, processes, structure, or practices of the organization. Only about 15 percent of the errors or complaints can be traced back to someone who didn't care or wasn't conscientious enough.

Frontline employees often provide excellent service to the customer in spite of, not because of, their organization's support and systems. Given the obstacles present in many organizations, it's a minor miracle that service is being provided at all! But that service is often being provided by caring employees who believe sincerely in the service they provide to the individual.

The assumption that "the workforce is to blame" is based in a common, but erroneous, inclination to place blame by asking *who* rather than *what* went wrong. The resulting organizational culture—a culture of fear, covering your backside, and finger-pointing—fixes blame rather than fixing the problem. If management really wants to find the source of declining service levels, the best place to start is with an honest look in the mirror and not at the individuals struggling daily to do their jobs.

Manager Alert

If management really wants to find the source of declining service levels, the best place to start is with an honest look in the mirror.

PERFORMANCE BY THE ORGANIZATION, TEAMS, AND THE INDIVIDUAL

Performance in an organization occurs at three levels: (1) the overall performance of the organization; (2) the performance of groups of individuals, whether as bureaus within an agency or as teams with a single focus per team; and (3) the performance of the individual employee.

The performance of each of these levels needs to be communicated externally to the customer and stakeholder and internally to the employee, but the degree of detail in the reporting varies widely. The overall performance of the organization should be a matter of public record. Achievement of the mission and strategic objectives generally are in annual performance reports and should also be part of the budget documents to let the taxpayer know what is achieved with the tax dollar.

Individual performance is not generally a matter of public record. An exception would be when someone does something truly outstanding and deserves special acknowledgment (for example, someone is instrumental in creating a partnership with an outside organization).

A job well done deserves to be acknowledged, so achievements should be shared. Not only does doing so serve to encourage and inspire other employees, it also shows the customer and stakeholder that the organization cares about its employees. But daily performance and achievement of established goals within the performance management process should remain part of the individual's private record.

The sharing of achievements and failures by the organization as a whole, or by groups of individuals, helps foster a new level of trust and communication. This is particularly important in the public sector. There has been a great deal of rhetoric about building the public trust. Polls showed that confidence in the government and in public-sector employees to "do the right thing" had dropped to an all-time low. With reengineering, reinvention, and the introduction of performance management, that confidence began to improve significantly. However, in today's world, that level of confidence has dropped amid political wrangling in Washington. Federal managers need to work closely with their customers, stakeholders, and partners to rebuild that trust.

Information technology can revolutionize measurement, and investments in information technology free employees to "work smarter." Government managers need timely access to accurate information. Public-sector employees with historical knowledge do not necessarily share that information with managers. Internal communication allows employees to become better professionals, make better decisions, deliver better customer service, meet performance goals, and contribute to an organization's success.

Keep in mind that what you measure is what you get. An organization's performance measurement system strongly affects the behavior of its managers and employees. Traditional financial accounting measures, if not considered as part of a larger picture of organizational achievement, can give misleading signals for continuous improvement and innovation—activities that today's competitive environment demands.

Many public-sector organizations have tested new kinds of measurement systems more appropriate for creating world-class performance. Most of these performance measures are not new but have been in use in the private sector for many years. What is new is that they can now drive daily operations and decision-making.

Here, too, balance is important. Financial measures provide the results of actions already taken. Operational measures complement the financial measures and drive future financial performance. Measures of customer satisfaction are important, but they should measure what an organization must do internally to meet customer expectations. In combination, these measures provide a balanced view of overall performance and bring together in a single report all the functions of a public-sector organization. A balanced approach to performance measurement forces management to consider whether improvement in one area may have been achieved at the expense of another.

In developing a performance measurement system, try not to choose between financial and operational measures. No single measure can provide a clear performance target or focus attention on the critical areas of the business. A balanced presentation of both financial and operational measures will provide a more complete picture of achievement.

Manager Alert

In developing a performance measurement system, try not to choose between financial and operational measures.

TOWN HALLS AND OTHER MEETING ALTERNATIVES

With the evolution of the Internet, it has become easy to discount the value of face-to-face encounters. Remember that not everyone has a computer or access to the Internet (without going to a local library). The National Partnership for Reinventing Government (NPR) began a program named "Conversations with America" to engage federal workers in two-way conversations with their customers—the American public—on how to improve customer service. A conversation can take place in many settings: town hall meetings, focus groups, electronic chat rooms, e-mail, customer surveys and comment cards, call-in radio and television shows, and toll-free call centers.

Technology can be useful for purposes of gathering information. Websites and chat rooms can provide meaningful dialogue but should not be the only communication methods used. The NPR categorized the methods used for Conversations with America into four areas:

- Face-to-face conversations (meeting personally with individuals or groups)
- Electronic conversations (computerized question and answer)
- Written conversations
- Telephone conversations.

In Chapter 3, the concepts of focus groups (a small number of individuals focused on a specific issue) and workshops (a large group of individuals, usually concerned with an issue internal to an organization) were discussed at length. Another venue is the town hall meeting. Town hall meetings are not a new concept. These meetings, based in part on the Quaker culture, have been held for centuries. The term now encompasses not only a group of individuals meeting in a specific location to discuss issues but also interested parties linked by technology such as media (e.g., local television channels or Internet discussion forums). The basic idea remains the same, however—to reach out to the public and actively seek their input into organizational decisions.

Written conversations, including customer surveys and comment cards, are an area where media (especially print media) can be very helpful. Individuals who do not have a computer may read a newspaper. Remember that seeking customer opinion marks a significant change in government culture and, although significant strides have been made in recent years, particularly through the efforts of organizations such as the NPR, there is still room for improvement.

Telephone conversations include not only the use of toll-free numbers but also call-in radio and television shows. Toll-free call centers using automated answering systems need to be designed and monitored carefully for ease of use.

COMMUNICATING INTERNALLY AND EXTERNALLY, AND WHERE TO DIFFERENTIATE

Communication is critical, but is it possible to be too open? Although the public sector may not be prone to "industrial espionage" in the strict interpretation of the term, some issues are inappropriate for public discussion, perhaps because they contain classified information or will invade an individual's right to privacy. Each organization must evaluate honestly what can be shared with the public and which needs should be kept internal to the management of the organization.

In making this decision, however, management also needs to keep in mind that the more open the organization can be with the public, the better the relationship will tend to be. Overall organizational achievements or failures, as well as team achievements, generally should be available for public review. Sometimes a team may fail to achieve a specific goal, but the learning experience leads to the development of a better process. Learning from one's mistakes shows the customer that the organization is trying.

THE NEED FOR HONESTY IN ESTABLISHING PUBLIC TRUST

Sharon Caudle, PhD, a Texas A&M University Bush School of Government and Public Service faculty member and former GAO team leader, is an expert in what are called *public governance responsibilities*. She argues that if public-sector organizations are to meet these responsibilities successfully, they must appear as policy and resource stewards to their stakeholders.

To this end, in evaluating performance plans and actual performance, the following questions must be answered, according to Caudle:

- Is the mission in line with mandates?

- Are key stakeholder needs and requirements understood and integrated?
- Are multiple or duplicate programs integrated for best policy results?
- Are mandated policies effectively translated to implementation goals?
- Are financial and investment performance restraints and expectations made clear?

The current political climate, including sequestration and the disagreements among the House, Senate, and administration, have damaged the public trust in public institutions. Accountability through disclosure, analysis, and dissemination can restore the public trust. Through open communication, the public can see what it is paying for and understand the results of management actions. Open communication, both internal and external, builds trust in the overall system, allows individuals and teams to shine, and restores faith in the capabilities of the organization.

Manager Alert

Open communication, both internal and external, builds trust in the overall system, allows individuals and teams to shine, and restores faith in the capabilities of the organization.

In 1998, Congress ordered the Internal Revenue Service (IRS) to begin a massive restructuring and reform effort to help restore public confidence in the American tax system. In restructuring, the IRS faced two major measurement challenges: (1) to translate their mission into measures that encourage desired performance and (2) to design measures that balance customer service focus with overall tax administration responsibilities. At the IRS, the distinction between customer and client is clear. The differences between previous approaches and the balanced approach now used at the IRS are shown in Table 5-2.

This new approach allowed the IRS to understand both the taxpayer's and the employee's point of view while assessing and improving quality. As a result of this approach and the resultant understanding, the IRS created an Office of Organizational Performance Management, which helps managers get closer to the work. Among the support activities for this are a tool kit for managers and multiple channels for feedback. The integrated operations plan and innovations are being given an opportunity to evolve in a less stressful environment, with temporary suspension of most reviews. The IRS realizes that organizational culture change takes time and has an evolving strategic planning process that addresses culture change.

Table 5-2
IRS Changes in Approach after
Application of Balanced Measures

Previous Approach	Balanced Approach
Emphasis on achieving measures	Emphasis on achieving mission
Dependent on dollar results	Balanced priorities
No customer or employee measures	New customer satisfaction and employee satisfaction measures
Large number of measures	Small number of measures
Process measures used	Outcome measures used
Measures intended to address every situation	Measures allow for managerial judgment
Measures driven to front of organization	Measures aggregated from front of organization
Minimal attention to quality	Quality considered equally with quantity
Offices ranked	No ranking of offices

"Communication is critical to the process throughout—from its inception, when you make the decision to create a scorecard, to the point in time where it is produced. You must have an open, honest dialogue regarding what it takes to get the job done."

—Chuck DeCoste, director of the Veterans Benefits
Administration's Data Management Office

Chapter 6

LEADING THE PUBLIC-SECTOR ORGANIZATION IN A CHANGING WORLD

Leadership does not—and cannot—stop at the top, but must cascade throughout an organization, creating champions and a team approach to achievement of the mission. Leadership by employees in solving problems and achieving the mission is what makes for a most successful organization.

In this chapter, this kind of leadership will be discussed in terms of the various roles that a leader should take to achieve it. A leader needs to be able to share the role—it is not realistic in today's world to take the "because I said so" approach. A leader should be an educator, because people respond better when they understand the reason for a decision. In the strategic planning process, a leader is an architect, working with a team to design the best and most productive organization. A leader is also a caretaker, watching over the organization, guiding it to a successful mission. Through example, a good leader establishes strong performance management principles.

As a leader of innovation in the public sector, you need to know the expectations of your stakeholders and the client, whether as a recipient of the benefit or service or as a taxpayer. What does the employee need to meet those expectations? Goals and objectives cannot be achieved without taking those expectations and needs into account. Most important, cascading leadership creates an environment in which each individual employee is aware of his or her role in the achievement of the departmental mission. A public-sector organization that has achieved this cultural change will have a sustainability that becomes ingrained in the fabric of the organization.

The challenge to management is to use flexibility to provide a solution to problems. Individuals may be rewarded for their achievements by being promoted into management-level positions. To become good managers, however, they need training in human resource issues. Managers must take responsibility for poor performers, think in terms of partnering, and use available tools to present information for analysis clearly and efficiently.

Leadership is a critical element marking successful organizations, both public and private. Cascaded throughout an organization, leadership gives the performance management process a depth and sustainability that survives changes at the top—even those driven by elections and changes in political party leadership.

> A boss creates fear; a leader, confidence. A boss fixes blame; a leader corrects mistakes. A boss knows all; a leader asks questions. A boss makes work drudgery; a leader makes it interesting. A boss is interested in him or herself; a leader is interested in the group.
>
> —Russell H. Ewing

Two experts in the field, the Honorable Maurice McTigue, a former New Zealand cabinet member now working at George Mason University, and Patricia Ingraham, PhD, of the Maxwell School at Syracuse University, emphasize in their teaching the importance of strong leadership in a political environment. Given the constraints such an environment can impose, a successful public-sector organization needs leadership that supports the adoption of balanced measures as a feature of organizational management and accountability.

A balanced set of measures allows leaders to think of their organization in its totality. There is no one "right" family of measures. The measures must reflect the overall mission and strategy of the organization but must drive the organization in its day-to-day activities. In most cases, they are developed through an iterative, evolutionary process. You can have as many categories as you want, but you should keep it as simple as possible so that your measurements can be global and quick.

There is no generic set of balanced measures that can be applied as a best practice to all functions of the public sector. Certain conditions, however, need to exist within any public-sector organization for a balanced approach to performance management to be successful:

- Strong leadership that supports the adoption of balanced measures as a feature of organizational management and accountability
- The capability to communicate effectively throughout the organization and the organization's ability to communicate to decisionmakers
- The knowledge that customers, employees, and stakeholders are fully informed and that they understand and support the initiatives of the organization.

SHARING THE LEADERSHIP ROLE

Without exception, successful organizations, both public and private, cite strong leadership as a key factor in their success in applying a balanced approach to performance management. Without support from senior management and top officials, it is difficult, although not impossible, to establish a successful strategic framework that integrates all the necessary factors.

Certain leadership truisms apply whether an organization's management structure is like a pyramid or more like a web, characterized by interconnections crisscrossing throughout the structure:

- Good leadership relies on good communication.
- All members of the organization must have clearly defined responsibilities.

Manager Alert

Good leadership relies on good communication.

The stereotypical "great leader" in our culture is the rugged individual, carving out a role and marching forward, the troops following faithfully (and blindly) behind. Unfortunately, this type of individual traditionally would focus on a short-term result rather than long-term goals and objectives. The best leaders

- Report back to the employees, customers, and other stakeholders
- Use self-assessment tools, such as the Baldrige criteria
- Involve the legislative branch through consultation or representation on working groups and committees
- Involve the customer, stakeholder, and employee at every phase of the management process
- Involve the unions early and often.

Today's public-sector organizations face relatively new concepts of strategic planning and accountability for the achievement of their missions. These responsibilities require a very different type of leader—one who can build an organizational consciousness. The "new" organization shares a common vision of the future, and individual employees work together to achieve that vision.

This process creates a natural tension between where the organization is now and where it wants to be. Peter M. Senge, Director of the Systems Thinking and Organizational Learning program at the MIT Sloan School of Management, likens this tension to a rubber band stretched between two hands. The lower of the two hands is where the organization is, and the upper hand is where it wants to be. To relieve the stress, either the reality has to be raised or the expectations lowered.

Today's leader must create that tension, which requires three distinct efforts. First, there has to be an accurate evaluation of the current status of the organization. This means a "reality check," perhaps based in a SWOT (strengths, weaknesses, opportunities, threats) assessment (see Chapter 3). To create an accurate picture, there needs to be feedback from everyone: customer and client (not always the same people), stakeholder, and employee. Second, a vision of the future has to be developed in consonance with the views of the same groups of individuals. The third element—communicating the first two elements throughout the organization—is the most vital and perhaps the most challenging.

This type of leadership allows individuals to move toward the goal, armed with the knowledge of the two ends of the spectrum. Unlike the traditional problem-solving methods, it does not wait for a crisis to react. It is a proactive, rather than reactive, method of development.

The roles of today's leader in the above process are threefold: educator, architect, and caretaker.

THE LEADER AS EDUCATOR

As an educator, today's leader helps every individual understand both the current reality and the vision for the future. As the vision evolves through discussions with stakeholders, customers, and employees, there should be an awareness of training or system changes that will be needed to achieve the future vision. What training does the individual employee need to do his or her job better? Do the organization's data systems provide accurate information in a timely manner so that the employee can make a well-informed decision? To achieve an organizational mission, the organization must be able to act in a unified manner. What is being done in your organization to cross-train individuals from different perspectives? Is your organization "stovepiped"? Remember that individual employees cannot fully comprehend their roles in the overall process unless and until they understand the process itself.

Education is also a vital part of the communication effort. Not only the employees need to know and understand individual roles and responsibilities—customers, clients, and stakeholders also need to be able to see the big picture and understand the challenges the organization may be facing in trying to achieve its mission. The role of the leader as educator in this phase is one of communicator. Stakeholders especially want to understand the challenges, and employees will look to the leader of the organization to see how he or she responds to questions. If the leader of the organization does not accept responsibility, then the employee will certainly be less likely to do so. The federal manager should lead by example.

THE LEADER AS ARCHITECT

For the organization to achieve a stated mission or vision, it must have a road map showing how to get from here to there. Earlier discussions in this book compared the approach to the flight panel on an airplane or the dashboard of a car. The same metaphors apply here. The airline may want the airplane to go at specific speeds and maintain certain rates of efficiency, but if the person who built the plane didn't do the job correctly, all the flight plans in the world will not make that plane capable. Alternatively, even though the speed limit is 65 miles per hour for many interstate roads and the driver of the car may want to reach a destination at a specific time, a car that was not designed correctly won't make it there on time.

Regardless of which metaphor you choose, a balanced approach allows you to consider all the important operational measures at the same time, letting you see whether improvement in one area is achieved at the expense of another. Key indicators should tell you how the organization is doing. They can change over time to reflect a shifting in emphasis for organizational goals. Performance levels can be reported on a monthly or quarterly basis. All levels of management, including field personnel, can participate in the reporting process; together, they provide a good idea of the health of the organization from a variety of perspectives. It is only with a balanced approach that leaders can create success throughout their organizations.

This proven approach to strategic management embeds long-term strategy into the management system through the mechanism of measurement, translating vision and strategy into a tool that effectively communicates strategic intent and motivates and tracks performance against established goals.

The architect of today's organization must establish the vision and core values by which the organization will function. Those concepts then translate into strategies that in turn determine day-to-day policy decisions. The architect cannot design this structure in a vacuum. If you were designing a house, you would consult with the people who will live in the house. By the same token, today's leader must involve customers, clients, stakeholders, and employees in the creation of a mission-oriented organization, focused on a unified vision for the future.

THE LEADER AS CARETAKER

Senge refers to this role as the "servant leader," a term also used by Robert Greenleaf in his book *Servant Leadership.*[1] Greenleaf states: "The servant leader is servant first . . . This conscious choice brings one to aspire to lead."[2]

Today's leader must tend to the employees; the organization itself; and its vision, mission, and goals. When an organization is undergoing reinvention, people are uncertain about their role in the "new" organization and, sometimes, whether their jobs are secure. In many cases, especially in the public sector, the concepts of accountability and responsibility are being redefined. Being held accountable for measures that may not be totally under an individual's control can cause anxiety. A leader needs to be aware of that potential for anxiety and use open lines of communication to assuage those fears.

Leadership that takes into account feedback from its employees, customers, and stakeholders, together with performance data, has a full scope of information upon which to make informed decisions. And it is a basic tenet of good management that the more informed the decision, the sounder that decision will be.

It verges on paradoxical that a good leader must be a catalyst who institutes a culture that will survive changes in leadership and administration. The key here is to cascade leadership throughout an organization and to give ownership of strategic plans and performance measures to career employees. That ownership, which involves organizational learning and culture change, is necessary for sustainability.

Manager Alert

A good leader must be a catalyst who institutes a culture that will survive changes in leadership and administration.

"You change culture by changing the conversation. The theory behind reinvention is that you must change the way people do their job in order to change the culture. At the same time, you must continually think about how this will be accomplished, while at the same time serving your customers."

—Morley Winograd, senior policy advisor to Vice President Al Gore and director of the National Partnership for Reinventing Government

ESTABLISHING STRONG PERFORMANCE MANAGEMENT PRINCIPLES

In leading organizational change, always keep in mind that good management is grounded in three fundamental principles: excellence, accountability, and timely action.

Expect Excellence

Federal managers should establish a set of balanced measures and communicate those expectations to the individual employee. The objective of this effort is to ensure that employees have a clear idea of what is expected of them. Feedback should be ongoing, rather than the once or twice a year that evaluations are scheduled. This type of open communication also alleviates some of the anxiety referred to above because the leader becomes a caretaker by constant feedback and communication.

Establish Accountability

Managers should be measured on how well they meet their responsibilities as leaders. Do managers focus rewards on real results? Are managers trained to be managers? This concept is quite new to the public sector. Individuals are traditionally promoted to positions of leadership within a division or program because they are good at their jobs. There is an innate fallacy here. Simply because people are good at their jobs (e.g., accounting or engineering), it does *not* mean that they will automatically be good managers.

To become a good manager requires training, and an organization that wants to achieve success has to be willing to spend the time and money to train its managers. People skills need to be developed, including how to establish and maintain an open line of communication and how to appraise performance. Good managers are not born; skills are developed through training and experience, neither of which stands alone.

Take Timely Action

Poor performance should be addressed early: Do not wait until it makes an impact on the organization. Early intervention, including training, counseling, and open communication, can prevent poor performance from becoming a major problem. Sharing best practices can also help. Rather than merely telling someone that he or she is doing something wrong, suggest trying another approach that has been successful elsewhere.

The Performance Management Contract plan asks agencies to draft performance agreements with the highest levels of departmental leadership for the next appraisal cycle. Those agreements would contain a balanced set of performance measures, dealing with customer satisfaction, employee involvement, and success in performance planning.

If the leadership of a public-sector organization works, it will result in internal and external support for organizational initiatives. Internally, ownership will be given to the employees, allowing each one to be a leader within his or her own sphere. For example, the Canadian St. Lawrence Seaway Management Corporation organizes its performance indicators according to a clearly delineated pyramid. All employees know where they fit into the structure and what they are expected to achieve.

Top-level support in successfully establishing a balanced set of measures can be seen in numerous organizations where this strong executive leadership has cascaded throughout the organization.

> The wicked leader is he whom the people despise.
>
> The good leader is he whom the people revere.
>
> The great leader is he of whom the people say, "We did it ourselves."
>
> —Lao Tsu

NOTES

1. Robert Greenleaf, *Servant Leadership: A Journey into the Nature of Legitimate Power and Greatness* (New York: Paulist Press, 1977).

2. Ibid, page 27.

Chapter 7

MAKING IT ALL WORK: BUILDING A STRATEGIC FRAMEWORK

The best strategic plan, if left to exist in a vacuum, will be meaningless. The plan must become an integral part of the daily operations of an organization, part of the overall business planning and budget planning functions. It must also be linked to your data systems to complete the strategic management framework

A balanced set of performance measures cannot be created in a vacuum. To be successful, you must involve *every* activity of your operations. Not only do you need to balance customer, stakeholder, and employee interests (keeping in mind that "balance" does not necessarily mean equal thirds), establish accountability, and determine the best means to collect and use data, but you also need to make these concepts work in practice.

Manager Alert

To be successful, you must involve *every* activity of your operations.

Translating a set of measures into achievement of organizational mission means connecting those activities being measured to the organization's daily operations. Although this is widely recognized in theory, practical application in the public sector has met with widely varied levels of success.

In Kaplan and Norton's Balanced Scorecard (BSC), the scorecard quadrants are linked with arrows representing the power and synergy of management action, that is, creating integration between the measures, action plans, and accompanying management action (Figure 7-1). Whether in the public-sector Government

Performance and Results Act (GPRA) framework or the private-sector strategic management framework, that integration is what allows managers to monitor cause-and-effect relationships and design proactive strategies.

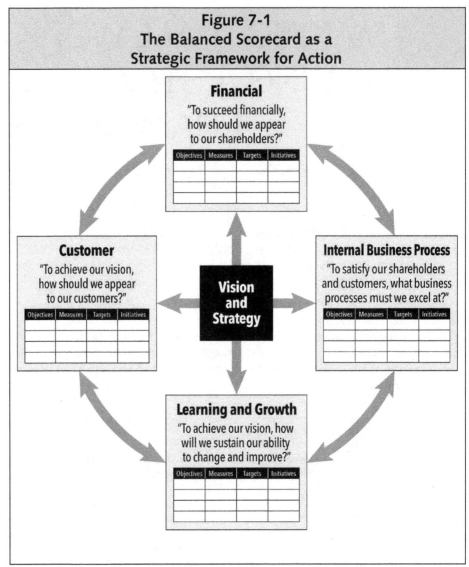

Figure 7-1
The Balanced Scorecard as a
Strategic Framework for Action

Source: Robert S. Kaplan and David P. Norton, "Using the Balanced Scorecard as a Strategic Management System," *Harvard Business Review* (January-February 1996): 77. Reprinted with permission.

Public-sector organizations that have been through at least two strategic planning cycles know from first-hand experience the importance of institutionalizing—and then integrating—processes. The key to driving actions and results is to connect all the critical elements:

- Connect to employees and customers
- Connect to the business plan
- Integrate with data systems
- Integrate with the budget process.

LINKING YOUR PLAN TO DAY-TO-DAY OPERATIONS

Connecting to your customers and employees is vital to the success of any performance planning, measurement, or management and is a driving concept within the BSC. If you try to manage the performance of your organization in a vacuum—that is, not seeking customer and employee input—you may succeed in the short term but are doomed to failure in the long term.

Involving your employee in the planning process makes him or her a part of the team. Moreover, communication translates to respect for the individual employee, an especially important consideration to public-sector employees, who are dedicated to their jobs and believe very firmly in the services they offer. They know what they need to get the job done right. Just ask them.

Working over a long period of time with working groups and commissions, state and local governments have connected with their customers and stakeholders to a much greater extent than has the federal sector. The latter has, however, made significant improvements in this area within the last two years. For most public-sector organizations, linking to customers and employees is the greatest challenge. Turning an entire organization into a seamless team involves culture change all the way from the head of the organization to the individual employee and customer. It takes communication and leadership. Best practices that link the employee and customer to the various phases of performance planning and management are described in detail in earlier chapters.

Manager Alert

Turning an entire organization into a seamless team involves culture change all the way from the head of the organization to the individual employee and customer.

LINKING YOUR PLAN TO THE BUSINESS PLAN

If an organization develops its business plan separately from its strategic plan or annual performance plan, managers and frontline workers alike will not know which set of performance measures actually count—that is, they won't know what they're supposed to be doing or what they're trying to accomplish, any more than will the organization as a whole. Business plans define the day-to-day outputs, inputs, and processes that make the organization function; these must be linked to the overall organizational mission and goals.

LINKING YOUR PLAN TO THE DATA SYSTEMS

The importance of having a minimal number of systems is a matter of efficiency as well as one of control and accountability. In working on linking systems together, consider an Enterprise Architecture (EA) process. (At this point in your reading, I can practically hear you groaning or see you rolling your eyes, but EA can be a very useful tool!) The EA process uses most of the steps we have already discussed, such as a SWOT (strengths, weaknesses, opportunities, threats) analysis and consultation with a broad range of system users. A successful EA effort will link your systems and/or create an interface among them. It helps focus efforts to improve communications among the organization and its partners, stakeholders and customers.

LINKING YOUR PLAN TO THE BUDGET PROCESS

Resources must be allocated on the basis of performance measurement and management. Otherwise, when a choice must be made between doing what is requested in a plan and doing what is needed to keep or obtain funding, the plan will always lose. Your budget must thus be inextricably linked to performance measures.

In *Performance Budgeting: Initial Experiences Under the Results Act in Linking Plans with Budget Experiences,*[1] GAO auditors reviewed 35 agencies' FY 1999 performance plans to determine how well their spending decisions were tied to their performance goals, as required under GPRA. The agencies with the best practices had performance plans that clarified how resources relate to results and had two things in common. First, these agencies used simple links between activities and goals. Second, they integrated budget justifications with performance plans.

Agencies must provide information on three levels of performance measures—strategic planning, budget planning, and performance measurement—thus making performance information a vital factor in justifying budget requests and in making executive and legislative branch funding decisions.

CREATING A STRATEGIC MANAGEMENT FRAMEWORK

If employees, customers, data, budgets, and results are all connected, you are well on your way toward having in place a successful strategic management framework. Such a framework creates an organization where achievement of a stated mission is clearly communicated throughout the organization and where everyone works toward the same goals and objectives.

Manager Alert

If employees, customers, data, budgets, and results are all connected, you are well on your way toward having in place a successful strategic management framework.

The U.S. Coast Guard and the Department of Veterans Affairs provide excellent examples of strategic management frameworks in the federal sector. The Coast Guard's "family of plans" illustrates the agency's strategic planning and strategic management architecture and has been recognized by the GAO as a best practice in strategic linkage. The architecture supports and institutionalizes the agency's measurement framework. The family includes the Coast Guard 2020 vision statement ("ready today, preparing for tomorrow"), the agency's strategic outlook, the commandant's direction, and the strategic plan. The strategic plan guides and directs (1) the agency performance plan and related annual budget request, (2) operational and support business plans, and (3) plans covering special areas, such as human resources and information technology. The field-produced regional strategic assessments provide input to the formulation of the strategic plan and directorate business plans.

The Veterans Administration's strategic plan is grounded in the notion of "One VA" that "delivers seamless service to veterans and their dependents." To this end, the department restructured the strategic planning and programs of its component elements (the Veterans Health Administration, the Veterans Benefit Administration, and the National Cemetery Administration) to function as a unified whole. Using state-of-the-art planning techniques, the department created a strategic planning process that will build a strong and resilient strategic base. Key components of that planning process include developing measures of program efficiency (i.e.., unit cost), measures of program outcomes, information systems that ensure that management data are available for each measure, benchmark levels of performance, mechanisms to link performance measurement to the budget, and mechanisms to link organizational goals and performance with individual employee goals and performance.

Strategic Framework and Coordination

A strategic framework and coordinated strategic outcomes provide the foundation for appropriately integrating the VA's research, policy development, and evaluation activities around its overarching strategic themes, including linking these to budget processes. It undertakes high-level analysis of emerging economic and social trends as a basis for developing and maintaining a future-oriented strategic policy guideline to assist the department in achieving its key objectives. This includes policy development, research and analysis (that crosses branch boundaries), providing expert advice and consultancy services to branches, and developing strategically focused budgetary processes and coordination.

For a coordinated strategic framework, the key objectives and strategies include

- Cooperatively developing and maintaining a strategic policy framework for the organization, in relation to the budget process, that reflects a systemic, behavioral, and cross-sector approach

- Working with other parts of the organization to develop policies that cross internal organizational boundaries (e.g., mutual obligations and simplification of processes)

- Refocusing research and evaluation activities across the organization (including through consultants and other externally funded organizations) to align them more closely to the overall strategic policy framework, in close consultation with other parts of the organization

- Ensuring a strong strategic focus to budget processes and proposals through extensive discussions, and developing better mechanisms for monitoring expenditure trends on programs

- Providing expertise and disseminating knowledge of broad social policy issues to relevant areas of the organization

- Developing close partnerships with internal and external stakeholders (across all strategic outcome groups, other departments, academic institutions, and the community sector) to foster shared understandings on strategic policy issues and assist the organization in achieving its objectives.

Thinking, as Well as Planning, Strategically

Most planners don't think strategically enough. They don't look far enough ahead or know how to read signs of what's coming. If they do, they don't think through the ramifications of their predictions and translate them into step-by-step procedures.

Studies by such organizations as GAO and the National Academy of Public Administration have consistently shown that organizations that undertake strategic planning enjoy significant improvements in effectiveness, efficiency, and productivity when compared to organizations that do not.

If leadership cascades throughout the organization, and performance management becomes an integral part of day-to-day operations, manager motivation and morale should improve. Properly done, performance management can instill a sense of satisfaction by giving managers a role in the creation of their own destiny. Managers will know what is expected of them; and when it is achieved, it can bring a sense of accomplishment.

Manager Alert

If leadership cascades throughout the organization, and performance management becomes an integral part of day-to-day operations, manager motivation and morale should improve.

When done correctly, a balanced approach to performance management should

- Create a workable road map for bottom-line results
- Make the most of time and limited resources
- Use a logical approach to unify the goals of the organization
- Improve the cost-effectiveness of programs
- Help an organization to serve customers and clients better
- Clarify the roles of every employee within the organization
- Write accurate, clear, and justifiable budgets
- Make communication clearer up and down the organization.

Consider These Variables

When putting together a strategic plan, many factors must be considered. Managing the complex internal activities of an organization is only part of the challenge.

The external environment—competitors, suppliers, government agencies, and customers (whose often inexplicable preferences must be anticipated)—poses one set of challenges. The interests of stakeholders, including owners, shareholders, employees, and the community-at-large, also have to be taken into account. Economic conditions, social change, political priorities, and technological developments, too, must be considered.

Beware of the Limitations

Of course, no one management approach is flawless, and a balanced approach has its limitations. It is not the answer to all managerial problems. External forces may not react as planned. Factors such as changes in economic activity or a sudden change in political environment are uncertainties that can affect the outcome of any plan.

A significant amount of time and other costs may be required for effective planning. This makes it important to apply a cost-benefit gauge to the process. Also remember that formal strategic planning is not designed to get an organization out of a current, sudden crisis. It may, however, help to avoid a comparable future crisis.

Do It Right

Performance management and measurement is hard work. It requires imagination, analytical ability, creativity, and fortitude. The size and nature of your organization will dictate the formality of the planning process. A large organization with diversified operations requires a more formal process than a smaller organization whose operations are less complex.

Do not discount the potential benefits of an outside consultant. Someone knowledgeable in the strategic planning process yet capable of objectivity in observing your organization can be important. By providing expertise and a fresh perspective, an outside expert can help you organize the planning process and guide you through it as smoothly as possible.

One Approach: The Strategic Planning Engine

Michael G. Dolence developed a concept called the Strategic Planning Engine (SPE), which links strategic decision-making with organizational key performance indicators. The SPE is most commonly used by educational organizations and provides a framework for making very complex and politically sensitive decisions in both friendly and hostile or uncooperative environments. The SPE can help an organization organize and use past information, including earlier planning and studies, and makes it unnecessary to reinvent the wheel.[2]

Although used predominantly in education, the SPE can help a complex organization make strategic decisions at all levels. It is a simple method to follow and use, so it works equally well for both small and large organizations. It provides a consistent framework that ties each of the levels together automatically while at the same time is effective at keeping diverse groups of decisionmakers focused on the most important elements of the organization's success.

The SPE can integrate activities already performed by the organization. Analysis and planning documents created as a result of an earlier management effort, such as Management By Objective, Zero-Based Budgeting, or Total Quality Management, may have already identified and defined a set of key performance indicators. These key performance indicators can be used as the basis for the new planning documents and may be merged with budget initiatives or program evaluations. Any elements of these types used in the overall planning and strategy development of an organization can be used in an SPE.

The SPE is designed to help all participating decisionmakers explore and understand fully the relationships between the organization, the objectives it seeks to achieve, and the environment. It is a method to help keep the organization aligned with its environment. Alignment is guided by the results of a cross-impact analysis that illuminates the impact of external and internal environmental strengths, weaknesses, opportunities, and threats on the organization's ability to achieve its goals and objectives. Brainstorming focuses on generating ideas that address all issues identified through the SWOT assessment. (For more information on the SWOT assessment, see Chapter 3.)

Developing a Strategic Framework

The following steps are recommended for the development of a strategic framework that links together the mission, goals, and indicators with the concepts of customer or client satisfaction and employee involvement and empowerment:

1. Develop key performance indicators.
2. Perform an external environmental assessment.
3. Perform an internal environmental assessment.
4. Perform a SWOT assessment.
5. Conduct brainstorming.
6. Evaluate the potential impact of each idea on each strength, weakness, opportunity, and threat.
7. Formulate strategies, mission, goals, and objectives.
8. Conduct a cross-impact analysis to determine the impact of the proposed strategies, goals, and objectives on the organization's ability to achieve its key performance indicators.
9. Finalize and implement strategies, goals, and objectives.
10. Evaluate the actual impact of strategies, goals, and objectives on organizational key performance indicators.

Figure 7-2 presents a suggested strategic framework.

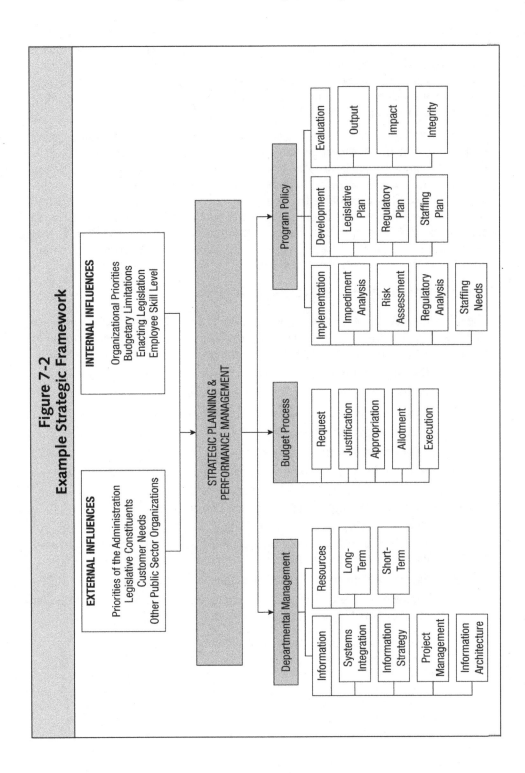

**Figure 7-2
Example Strategic Framework**

Workshops

In following these steps, some organizations find it helpful to conduct a workshop. A workshop should be at least one day in length, but not more than three days. Some of the roles that need to be filled for a workshop are

- A keynote speaker (30 to 60 minutes) to walk everyone through the overall process and set the tone
- A navigator/architect who can consult with the executive team, helping them to develop and implement a strategic planning framework
- An evaluator who can assess the effectiveness of the current strategic plan, as well as any processes
- A coach who can work with teams to develop and implement strategic planning across all levels of the organization
- A retreat facilitator who can design a strategic planning retreat and can serve as facilitator for any planning sessions.

Strategic planning is not—and never will be—an easy process. To work well, it must be an integral part of the organization. However, if it is done well, your organization will thrive and achieve success.

> You've got to think about "big things" while doing small things, so that all the small things go in the right direction.
>
> —Alvin Toffler

NOTES

1. United States General Accounting Office (GAO), *Performance Budgeting. Initial Experiences Under the Results Act in Linking Plans with Budgets* (Washington, DC: GAO, April 1999; AIMD/GGD-99-67). Available at www.gao.gov/assets/230/227280.pdf.
2. For more information on this concept, please refer to www.mgdolence.com.

Chapter 8

A FEW FINAL WORDS

I hope you have enjoyed this book and found it helpful. Please keep in mind, however, that there are a lot of really good business practices out there but no "one size fits all" approach. Each organization is different, whether in the service it provides, the product it creates, or simply the size and culture of the organization as a whole. Never try to force the practices of another organization onto your own—always remember to *adapt,* don't *adopt.*

In other words, maintaining a balanced approach does not necessarily mean applying the Balanced Scorecard to your organization. It does mean that, as a manager, you keep in mind all aspects of your organization when setting future strategies and goals.

Consultation is an iterative and critical process in the development of a solid strategic plan. Although the definition of customer and stakeholder may be blurred in the public sector (often the same groups will be both stakeholder and customer), a manager needs to keep in mind that the public sector organization exists because of its responsibilities to customers and stakeholders. Be aware of, and listen to, their expectations.

A key part of an organization's strategy is its communication plan. Even though you may not be able to share all of your strategies (e.g., classification issues may prevent some ideas from being made public), do try to share what you can. Share performance data on a quarterly basis when possible.

Organizational leaders have multiple responsibilities that pull them in several directions on a daily basis. As a manager, be aware of that and try to keep your leadership briefed on changes as they occur. Make sure they know what is being communicated to the public so they are not blindsided. Work with them to communicate their goals for the organization while communicating the expectations of partners, customers and stakeholders to leadership.

Performance *management* cannot exist without performance *measurement.* As a popular saying has it, "what gets measured gets done." Well, yes, but you may not be measuring the right thing. If your departmental function is law enforcement, you may think you want to measure the number of arrests—but that number alone is meaningless. If the number of arrests goes up, is it because you are doing a better job of enforcement or because more crimes are being committed? If the number goes down, is it because your organization is doing a poor job of enforcing laws— or a better job, so that people are less likely to commit crimes? Measures need to be reviewed and challenged throughout the performance period to be sure that what is being measured aligns with departmental goals.

Two other examples of this dichotomy are health and education. Although student academic performance is measured in schools, it doesn't improve the quality of teaching unless the data is applied to system improvements. We measure virtually every aspect of the health of individuals but it doesn't change access to and quality of care. Leadership has to be willing to apply lessons learned to a process of continuous improvement—otherwise, measurement produces only meaningless numbers.

Last, but not least, it all has to work together, which is not as easy as it may sound. You can create the best strategic plan in history, but if it doesn't link to what the employee does on a daily basis, it will not work.

This book does not purport to be a complete survey of the topics of strategic planning and performance management, but rather an attempt to provide guidelines to help managers in their efforts.

There are many more great ideas out there! See the References and Resources section for further online reading to get you started in thinking strategically.

CASE STUDIES

The following case studies offer examples of successful and ongoing application of the principles of strategic planning.

SOCIAL SECURITY ADMINISTRATION

The Social Security Administration (SSA) is an independent federal agency with approximately 65,000 employees. SSA is committed to both the concepts of the Government Performance and Results Act of 1993 (GPRA) and to improving its ability to manage for results on a day-to-day basis at all levels of the agency.

Strategic Planning Process

SSA has ongoing executive sponsorship for each strategic objective, with an internalized process for sponsorship accountability. Process owners and champions are identified throughout the planning process. The Office of Strategic Management developed a planning guide to help support strategic management within the agency.

The strategic management focus is on programs for objective achievement (POAs). A POA is a written plan identifying a set of strategies and "key initiatives" proposed by an executive sponsor (or team of co-sponsors) that lead to the achievement of a strategic objective. The POA reflects the GPRA focus on results and ensures that SSA's activities are tied directly to its agency strategic plan and annual performance plans. Budget and IT system resources are allocated to those initiatives. This strategic management framework and process allows SSA to evaluate and act upon the plans, actions, and performance measures and targets on an ongoing basis.

Establishing a Balanced Set of Measures

SSA has used a large number of output measures since becoming one of the GPRA performance plan pilot sites in 1994. SSA created a workgroup to develop a performance measurement framework and strategic goals, focusing on what was most important for the public and for customers.

During the pilot phase, SSA developed a performance measurement framework that initially aligned with three strategic goals and ultimately broadened into a balanced set of measures and five strategic goals: responsive programs, world-class service, best-in-business management, values employees, and public understanding. SSA has used a variation of the balanced scorecard concept since 1994.

In developing its first GPRA agency strategic plan, SSA's executive staff stated that the agency's mission was "to promote the economic security of the nation's people through compassionate and vigilant leadership in shaping and managing America's social security programs," and then went on to develop the current five strategic goals and objectives.

SSA's five strategic goals and objectives cut across all programs and encompass all of the agency's administrative activities:

1. To promote valued, strong, and responsive social security programs and conduct effective policy development, research, and program evaluation

2. To deliver customer-responsive, world-class service

3. To make SSA program management the best in the business, with zero tolerance for fraud and abuse

4. To be an employer that values and invests in each employee

5. To strengthen public understanding of the social security programs.

SSA's planning process includes the development of POAs, which identify the needed resources and link them with the performance targets.

With the focus of planning on performance, the major criterion for approval or continuation of key initiatives is the extent to which they contribute to the achievement of agency strategic objectives. Accordingly, the executive staff considers proposed initiatives based on whether a compelling business case for a proposed or existing initiative has been presented. The business case answers the key question, "Why should SSA do this initiative, in terms of the cost and the intended benefits?" Benefits are presented in terms of the contribution of the initiative to achievement of one or more strategic objectives.

Accountability

An executive sponsor or team of co-sponsors manages each strategic objective. Sponsors are accountable for achieving progress against measurable results and ensuring the integration of agency activities necessary to achieve the goal. They are responsible for developing POAs to include development of objectives, performance indicators, annual and long-range performance targets, identification of the gap between current and target performance, proposal of strategies and initiatives to close the gap, and establishment of a team to manage achievement of the objectives.

SSA's approach to accountability is still evolving, but its purpose is clear: to ensure that progress is being made toward meeting the agency's strategic goals and objectives. The approach includes several mechanisms that collectively keep the agency on track:

- **Quarterly performance reviews.** Once per quarter, SSA executives from across the agency meet to assess performance in various agencywide business processes. In these sessions, particular emphasis is on strategic objectives that affect field operations.

- **Additional performance reviews.** Additional reviews may be held as needed to focus on progress in accomplishing agency performance goals. Topics may also include setting or reconsidering short-range performance indicators or targets, issues needing resolution that have been raised by executives about individual objectives they sponsor, and introduction of new key initiatives.

- **Monthly tracking of performance.** SSA has an executive management and information system that provides a library of agency-level performance information used by SSA's executive staff to make decisions.

Many SSA components and individuals are involved in the planning process in support of the executive staff and POA sponsors. These include, among others, component planning representatives, component budget analysts, and key initiative team leaders. A budget analyst is assigned to each objective and each key initiative.

Data Collection and Reporting

The objective sponsor is responsible for assuring that a measurement system is in place to yield valid and reliable measures of performance and to identify a timetable for assessing performance.

Performance data for quantifiable measures are generated by automated management information and workload measurement systems as a byproduct of routine operations. The performance level for several indicators relating to the accuracy of SSA's processes and public satisfaction comes from surveys and workload samples designed to achieve very high levels (usually 95 percent confidence level) of statistical validity. Customer input comes from a variety of sources, including market measurement surveys, focus groups, comment cards, and feedback to websites. Employee input comes from a variety of sources, including employee satisfaction surveys and focus groups.

Each performance indicator is documented with its strategic goal, strategic objective, objective sponsor, definition, use, data source and contact, frequency of reporting, and validity and reliability. The monthly status of the performance indicators is available to sponsors and their staff on the executive management and information system intranet site.

Analysis and Review

An integrated evaluation plan ensures that each strategic goal, objective, and agency business process is appropriately evaluated to assess performance. It also ensures that there is no duplication in the evaluation processes and that the proper evaluations are being conducted.

Collecting, Evaluating, and Reporting to Customers and Stakeholders

Customers receive a pamphlet on achievement of customer service standards, *Reports to Customers*. The agency's strategic plan, annual performance plans, and accountability report are available to customers on the SSA's website.

Employees have access to these same plans and reports on the intranet site.

The strategic measurement framework ensures links between the body of 64 key initiatives with the goals and objectives in the strategic plan and the annual performance plan. Key initiatives are considered agency priorities and are therefore afforded a high priority in determining the work of the Office of the Deputy Commissioner, Systems (or Systems Office). Key initiatives' designations (as Tier 1, Tier 2, or Tier 3) affect the level and timing of the Systems Offices' commitment to support them.

During the development of the agency's annual budget, the executive staff makes investment decisions focused on how best to support the agency's strategic priorities. Objective sponsors then consider the impact of these budget decisions, especially concerning key initiatives, on their performance targets.

Best Practices/Enablers

Some best practices SSA identified were

- True leadership by the executives. Participation by the executive staff in the development of the performance measures for which they will be accountable helps to create ownership. They must be clear about expectations and true champions of the performance objectives they sponsor. However, this is an iterative process of change.
- Quarterly executive management meetings. Quarterly management meetings at which objective sponsors report are an effective mechanism to support accountability for performance.
- The planning guidance document. The Office of Strategic Management develops an annual guidebook that describes an overview of the planning

framework and guides the development and management of agency plans. It provides a consistent process for staff to follow and reduces the learning curve. The planning guide helps drive strategic management throughout the agency.

- Knowledge. It helps to continue to train and orient employees at all levels on the strategic planning process. Training and technical support are continually provided to professional staff involved in performance management. The agency also distributes the annual performance plan (to all who work at the headquarters and to all managers) and the Strategic Plan as a reference tool for day-to-day work.

- Customer focus. This is the underpinning of agency planning.

- Budget and planning post-mortems. These meetings identify planning and budget process improvements for the next annual cycle.

Lessons Learned

A summary of lessons follows:

- Change is hard, but the more you involve and communicate, the more quickly change occurs.

- Executives are busy with near-term management. It is important to make the strategic management process as painless as possible so they can also effectively focus on the long term, for which staff involvement and support are key.

- Because the program experts in the area you are measuring will be held accountable, they need to be involved.

- Champions and process owners are an integral part of the planning process. For performance to be used to manage, there needs to be a tie-in to systems and budgeted resource allocation.

- Coordination is needed at the executive and staff levels. You must have executive ownership and involvement. Staffs do what their bosses are interested in and what is measured.

Conclusion

The SSA found success through

- Leadership involvement and accountability. Executive sponsorship for each strategic objective, with an internalized process for sponsorship accountability.

- Communication. Internal (planning guidance documentation to support strategic management within the agency, including employees access to all plans and reports on the intranet site) and external (pamphlet on achievement of customer service standards and SSA's strategic plan, annual performance plans, and accountability reports available to customers on SSA's Internet website).

- Balanced measures. Goals and objectives that encompass all of the agency's administrative activities.

- Accountability and performance management. Frequent performance reviews by a sponsor who is responsible for assuring that a measurement system is in place to (1) yield valid and reliable measures of performance and (2) identify a timetable for assessing performance.

VETERANS BENEFITS ADMINISTRATION

The Department of Veterans' Affairs is composed of three organizational elements: (1) the Veterans' Health Administration, (2) the National Cemetery Administration, and (3) the Veterans' Benefits Administration (VBA). The VBA deals with housing, insurance, compensation, pensions, education, vocational rehabilitation, and counseling for veterans. The compensation area takes care of monthly payments to veterans for disabilities related to military service and to dependents in event of a veteran's death. The pension area addresses monthly payments to veterans or surviving dependents. Educational benefits are for service members and veterans after separation from service, as well as active reservists. Vocational rehabilitation and counseling rehabilitation services help disabled veterans obtain and keep employment or severely disabled veterans to gain a level of independence in their daily living. Housing at the VBA helps veterans with credit assistance in becoming homeowners, and insurance provides life insurance for service members and veterans. Nationally, there are 57 regional offices, with nine service delivery networks to accomplish the mission and goals recently created.

Establishing a Balanced Set of Measures

In the 1980s through 1990s, the Philadelphia office of the VBA started actively using Total Quality Management. Joe Thompson, former Under Secretary for Benefits and leader of the VBA, was involved in the process there. He later moved to the New York office, where GPRA brought about the balanced scorecard concept. In that office, they expanded stakeholder involvement beyond OMB and Congress to include veterans and taxpayers.

The New York office became an National Partnership for Reinventing Government (NPR) Reinvention Lab. As a result, that office provided the skeleton of key measures that the VBA modified and now uses. These key measures are speed, accuracy, cost, customer satisfaction, and employee development. The Balanced Scorecard (BSC) began as part of the VBA's nationwide efforts to comply with GPRA. Senior officials, staff managers, line managers, customers (indirectly), stakeholders, employees, labor partnerships, and contractors were all involved in developing the BSC.

A committee was formed from regional office and central office senior managers. Their initial goal was to ensure that compliance with GPRA was not merely a bureaucratic exercise but rather the establishment of a process that would be beneficial to the VBA as a whole. The performance measures that they defined were measures that would have meaning across all their business lines. The BSC provided the framework for this, and the committee did process mapping—defining what every business line does, describing exactly how they do it, and identifying performance gaps. This steering committee developed business plans for each one of the business lines and began integrating the budget into these plans. Thompson, who had been a member of the original committee representing the New York regional office, became the Under Secretary at the VBA and helped develop a road map for change.

In December 1997, Thompson conducted a series of planning sessions. Prior to this, the measures used were internal and did not take into account customer satisfaction. In January 1998, the *Road Map to Excellence* was developed and a BSC Team formed. In June of that year, the Data Management Office (DMO) was formed. Its role is to provide a centralized location for data warehousing.

In April 1999, the VBA published an electronic BSC on its intranet. Thompson views this step as one of the first steps in an iterative process designed to improve performance. The VBA has a balanced scorecard consistent with the basic framework of Kaplan and Norton. Although some of the measures are still in development, the VBA has the four basic categories of measures: financial (unit cost), internal (timeliness and accuracy), customer satisfaction and learning, and growth (employee development).

Measuring Performance—Data Collection and Reporting

The performance information used to be e-mailed to the field offices, but the VBA began to use the intranet in November 1998, ensuring that everyone has access to a consistent set of information. The service delivery networks use the intranet and the performance information on the balanced scorecard for day-to-day management decisions. They do not, however, use the performance information on the intranet as a grading tool. Source data for each measure is included on the site, and the data is very visible and available to all employees.

Currently, data warehouse technology is used to gather data and generate the balanced scorecard and supporting reports. This feature was enhanced to allow users to query directly against the data warehouse to generate ad hoc queries and reports.

Although the general public does not see the VBA balanced scorecard, it is available to employees, and the measures are available to the general public through departmental annual performance plans.

Analyzing and Reviewing Performance Data

The DMO is responsible for collecting and compiling the data and for producing and publishing the balanced scorecard. The DMO, business lines, and Office of Field Operations work in partnership to analyze the data.

Evaluating, Using, and Reporting Performance Information to Customers and Stakeholders

Fiscal Year 1999 was the first year the BSC was used, and it was a major transition within the VBA. Offices track the BSC at their level (service delivery networks, regional offices, and divisions in regional offices), and some tracking is also done at the team level. Every six weeks to two months, VBA leadership meets to review the BSC at each level (national, regional, and service delivery networks). Service delivery networks meet at least quarterly to discuss their performance.

The VBA holds BSC "summits" for midterm review and input from the field stations. The issues and proposed solutions gathered from this summit are aggregated by the DMO into four areas:

1. Administrative issues
2. Field issues/concerns
3. Service/business line issues/concerns
4. Completing the "to be determined" items on the balanced scorecards.

Links Between the Strategic Plan and Resource Allocation

Each of the balanced scorecard strategic objectives is contained in the business line plans, which the VBA has integrated with its budget submission. All scorecard measures are therefore linked to resource requests. The linking of resources directly with the performance objectives in a balanced approach is a significant challenge. It requires a mature process and experience with the scorecard and performance budgeting in order to form a direct link between scorecard performance and resources. This is not an issue unique to the VBA but is important throughout the public sector.

Benchmarking

Because the VBA is very similar to a commercial company, it benchmarked with similar insurance companies and organizations in several areas, e.g., telephone times and money to beneficiaries (disbursements). They also use some NPR-suggested benchmarks for standards. The VBA is developing a website to share best practices.

Lessons Learned

Two factors were instrumental for the VBA in implementing the BSC: flexibility and communication. The structure of the BSC, like all strategic planning processes, is iterative, and the established process must be flexible enough to work not only for headquarters but also for the field offices, while simultaneously allowing for comparisons among offices. The DMO makes the national data easily accessible for both national use and further analysis. The consistency that results from this type of warehousing results in every employee seeing the same information. Another facet of flexibility at the VBA is that measures are universal, but the weight given to each measure may differ among business lines. The BSC provides the framework, but there is flexibility within that framework to make it work for the individual organization.

The VBA found that communication, both internal and external, was also critical to the success of the BSC. Employees need to know where they fit into the process, and customers and stakeholders can use the BSC approach to understand the goals and processes of the organization. Communication is also used to build consensus within the organization as to what was to be measured and reported. Initial analysis of what had been measured historically at the VBA showed that the old systems did not measure the three most important groups: veterans, employees, and taxpayers. The employee development measures were the most difficult to develop. The unions were involved in developing them; they always have an interest in education issues for employees. In the education program area, they may have the first fully-developed employee measure in a skills matrix in New York that the VBA now uses as a model for development for all VBA employees. The score for employee development is determined by the number of employees who have the skills the organization needs to deliver service. The VA conducted a departmentwide employee survey in 1997 and an internal survey for employees during FY 1999. The department-wide survey data serves as a baseline. The education program's measures were more natural and easy to develop.

Other lessons learned as a result of the BSC process discussed include
1. The customer demands measuring performance.
2. The BSC allows better measurement against private industry.
3. The BSC leads to more collaboration in the whole organization.
4. The BSC forces a more holistic view of work.
5. The BSC provides a clear message to the field from headquarters.
6. The BSC allows easy view of your progress.
7. Most important, strong senior leadership is key to the development of the BSC in an organization.

Conclusion

VBA found success through

- Balanced measures. Financial (unit cost), internal (timeliness and accuracy), customer satisfaction and learning, and growth (employee development).

- Communication. Recognition that communication is critical to the process throughout—from its inception (when you make the decision to create a scorecard) to the point when it is produced.

- Alignment. Strategic objectives are linked to organizational functions and integrated with its budget submission and resource requests.

- Flexibility. Strategic planning process is iterative and is flexible enough to work for both headquarters and field offices, while simultaneously allowing comparisons among offices.

- Performance measurement. Departmentwide survey data serve as a baseline.

HOUSING AND URBAN DEVELOPMENT

When Andrew Cuomo took over as Secretary of Housing and Urban Development in 1993, he faced the challenge of restoring the reputation of a department. HUD's reputation was one of mismanagement at best and malfeasance at worst. Secretary Cuomo set out to change HUD and restore the public's trust in a department established to serve America's neediest populations.

To achieve this, he would need to accomplish a major transformation of the department's programs and management operations according to these defining principles:

- No "givens"
- Distinct business lines with the core purpose of each organization within HUD
- Need to match workload with workforce and skill with service
- Measure and reward performance
- Create changes with most leverage
- Examine privatization opportunities
- Master and utilize new technologies.

Extensive consultations were held with customers and stakeholders at all levels. One of HUD's challenges is that their product delivery frequently occurs through third parties (e.g., state and local governments or community groups). The way

HUD delivers its services and the speed of its processing affect these third-party capabilities.

Major dysfunctions were identified by "change agents" (i.e., employees/customers):

- Proliferation of boutique programs
- Organization by program rather than function
- Emphasis on process rather than performance
- Mismatched workload and workforce
- Management information systems not integrated, accurate, reliable, or timely
- Ineffective relationships between headquarters and field
- Confusing mandates for workforce
- Stewardship of public funds not a priority

As a result of this consultation effort, primary management reforms were set into motion:

- Reorganizing by function rather than program; consolidating or privatizing
- Modernizing/integrating HUD's outdated financial management systems
- Creating enforcement authority with one objective: restoring public trust
- Refocusing and retraining HUD's workforce to carry out the revitalized mission
- Establishing performance-based systems for HUD programs, operations, and employees
- Replacing HUD's top-own bureaucracy with a new, customer-friendly structure.

Keeping in mind the primary responsibility of the department, the HUD mission became twofold: (1) to empower people and communities, and (2) to restore the public trust.

The secretary set out its primary objectives based on HUD's business lines, and, having established these objectives, HUD set about to restructure itself to deliver services in a more efficient and effective manner. Six strategic objectives, based in the strategic planning process, were established:

- Fight for fair housing
- Increase affordable housing and home ownership
- Reduce homelessness
- Promote jobs and economic opportunity

- Empower people and communities
- Restore public trust.

The department established a business and operating plan that has allowed it to link the daily operations of HUD with the strategic goals and objectives stated in the departmental planning documents, including the strategic plan, the annual performance plan, and the budget submissions. The operating plan is the prime directive for work planning and management in department. The development process included review and examination of

- HUD's mission
- HUD's customers
- Programs, products, and services
- Processes and links across major program operations and organizations.

The next steps that were taken included:

- Align strategic objectives with
  o Major management reforms
  o New organizations
  o Operations
  o Programs
  o Services
- Develop quantitative goals at all levels of program delivery
- Develop a workload planning and customer service delivery approach.

Conclusion

HUD found success through

- Leadership. The secretary set out primary objectives based on HUD's business lines, then worked with departmental management to restructure the agency to deliver services in a more efficient and effective manner.
- Alignment. Quantitative goals were set at all levels of program delivery. The department linked the daily operations of HUD with the strategic goals and objectives stated in the departmental planning documents, including the strategic plan, annual performance plans, and budget submissions.
- Performance management. Refocusing and retraining HUD's workforce to carry out the revitalized mission. Establishing performance-based systems for HUD programs, operations, and employees.
- Consultation. Extensive consultations were held with customers and stakeholders at all levels.

ACRONYMS AND ABBREVIATIONS

BLM	Bureau of Land Management
BSC	Balanced Scorecard
CFO Act	Chief Financial Officers Act of 1990, Public Law 101-576
CIO Act	Information Technology Management Reform Act of 1996 (also known as the Clinger-Cohen Act or the CIO Act), Public Law 104-106
EA	Enterprise Architecture
FMFIA	Federal Managers Financial Integrity Act of 1982, Public Law 97-255
GAO	Government Accountability Office (before 2004, the General Accounting Office)
GMRA	Government Management Reform Act of 1994, Public Law 103-356
GPRA	Government Performance and Results Act of 1993, Public Law 103-62
GPRA 2010	Government Performance and Results Modernization Act of 2010, Public Law 111–352
IAM	Intangible Assets Monitor
IT	Information technology
NPR	National Partnership for Reinventing Government
OMB	Office of Management and Budget
SLSMC	St. Lawrence Seaway Management Corporation
SPE	Strategic Planning Engine
SWOT	Strengths, weaknesses, opportunities, threats
TQM	Total Quality Management

REFERENCES AND RESOURCES

Barnat, Ryszard. *Introduction to Strategic Management*. 2005. Available at: www.introduction-to-management.24xls.com.

Calkins, Tim. *Implementing Public Sector Performance Management: A Balanced Scorecard Approach* [conference paper]. Cary, NC: SAS Institute, Inc., 2001. Available at: http://www2.sas.com/proceedings/sugi25/25/ad/25p026.pdf.

Civic Research Alliance. Current Topics page: Municipal Strategic Planning. Mechanicsburg, PA: Civic Research Alliance. Available at: www.civicresearchalliance.com/currenttopics/001.php.

Edwards, Lauren M. *Strategic Planning in Local Government: Is the Promise of Performance a Reality?* [dissertation]. Atlanta, GA: Georgia State University, 2012. Available at: http://digitalarchive.gsu.edu/cgi/viewcontent.cgi?article=1037&context=pmap_diss.

Heinrich, Carolyn J. *Improving Public-Sector Performance Management: One Step Forward, Two Steps Back?* [conference paper]. Lawrence, KA: Public Management Research Association, 2003. Available at: www2.ku.edu/~pmranet/conferences/georgetownpapers/Heinrich.pdf.

International City/County Management Association (ICCMA). *New Framework for Public Sector Performance Management Helps Local Governments Improve Results During Tough Times*. Washington, DC: ICCMA, 2010. Available at: http://icma.org/en/icma/newsroom/highlights/Article/100433/New_Framework_for_Public_Sector_Performance_Management_Helps_Local_Governments_Improve_Results_durin.

Kwan, Myungjung. *Strategic Planning Utilization in Local Governments: Florida City Governments and Agencies* [dissertation]. Tallahassee, FL: Florida State University, 2006. Available at: http://diginole.lib.fsu.edu/cgi/viewcontent.cgi?article=3096&context=etd.

Municipal Research and Services Center of Washington (MRSC). *Strategic Planning*. Seattle, WA: MRSC, 2013. Available at: www.mrsc.org/subjects/governance/strategic.aspx.

Office of Financial Management, State of Washington. *Strategic Plan Guidelines*. Olympia, WA: Office of Financial Management, 2012. Available at: www.ofm.wa.gov/budget/instructions/operating/StrategicPlanGuidelines.pdf.

Office of the New York State Comptroller. *Local Government Management Guide: Strategic Planning.* Albany, NY: Office of the State Comptroller, 2003. Available at: www.osc.state.ny.us/localgov/pubs/lgmg/strategic_planning.pdf.

Poister, Theodore H. "The Future of Strategic Planning in the Public Sector: Linking Strategic Management and Performance." *Public Administration Review* 70, s1 (December 2010): s246–s254. Available at: www.ou.edu/cls/online/LSHA5113/pdfs/unit3_poister.pdf.

Young, Richard D. *Perspectives on Strategic Planning in the Public Sector.* Columbia, SC: University of South Carolina Institute for Public Service and Policy Research, 2005. Available at: www.ipspr.sc.edu/publication/perspectives%20on%20Strategic%20Planning.pdf.

INDEX